EIGHT HUSBANDS
& OTHER LOVERS

BOOK ONE
1955 to 1975

R. J. BUCKLEY

D1519460

DEDICATION

Much love to my brood of four:
Barry, Tami, Micheal, Mark,
and I apologize for your innocence being tainted
by my extensive collection of
husbands & other lovers.

CONTENTS

Marriage taught me to live alone.

Unknown

God created sex,
Priests created marriage.

Voltaire Quotes

Marriage is a great institution,
But I am not ready for an institution.

Mae West

Politics doesn't make strange bedfellows,
Marriage does.

Groucho Marx

Love is one long sweet dream,
And marriage is the alarm clock.

Unknown

Prologue

FROM ME TO YOU ...

Many of you have asked about my eight husbands and other lovers. Who was my favorite? Which one do I think was my soulmate? Why did I marry so many times? All are good questions. The answers I've given much thought to over the last few years. So, I finally agreed to bravely write the true story of the men in my life, about the husbands and other lovers. A story spanning over sixty years is quite lengthy for memoir, I know, compared to the description of a standard memoir, but it isn't an autobiography either. I am not writing my life story, only writing about those I married, and the lovers I didn't. To me it is memoir.

But it has not been an easy story to write because of the numbers, as you can imagine – the years and the many men. Therefore, to give me a respite in my attempt to re-live and remember all the important relationships, I've split it into four books, rather than one thick book. The complexity of it would be too much for me to write all at once. It would be most incredibly daunting, and I fear I'd give it up and return to my fiction, never to write the 900-page book that would take 25 hours to read. You, as the reader, might tire of reading and put it back on the shelf, never again to reopen it.

Indeed, publishing it in four books – each including two husbands and lovers of that timeframe – is the best solution for all. A 'series' if you will. Like one of the dramatic series that we all love with seasons and episodes. Consider each of these books a season, the chapters as episodes. Except you can read an entire "season" in one sitting, if you want, and you don't have to wait a week between episodes. And there will be books 2, 3, and 4 available soon.

I've used bits and pieces of my life in my fiction, but this memoir series is specifically of my actual husbands and lovers. A true story, no fiction, which has been quite the foreign endeavor for me. (I use first names and last initials.) But I've found it pleasant to write memoir, when recalling the good parts. Unpleasant at the same time because I'd have to dredge up the bad memories and relive them all over again. And being a memoir, I've been faced with having to write it in such a way that the story is compelling, believable, and hopefully relatable and beneficial to readers, but not hurtful to those who were on the sidelines, now reading about their dear loved ones. However, I may have crossed the line by not omitting wounding incidents, perpetrated by "him" or me, that pertain to the story. Remember, I reveal my wicked and flawed side too. Telling it as honest and as it was and is. I've said before and will say again, *truth is harder to write than fiction.*

All eight of my husbands have passed on, and some of the lovers too. Consequently, in writing in complete honesty, I must warn you I've touched on some unpleasantness. Still, I apologize in advance if I've not always taken the high road - which is my intention … but we all know with mountain peaks and hills, there are valleys, caves, crevices and deep dark holes, even sink holes … in all our lives and psyche.

PLEASE NOTE: I swear that this series of four books shall contain the truth, the whole truth, nothing but the truth as I recall, so help me God! And my truths are the only living memory of the relationships.

Thank you for trusting and believing in me.

R J Buckley 2022

EIGHT HUSBANDS
& OTHER LOVERS

BOOK ONE
1955 to 1975

R. J. BUCKLEY

"Memory is the Mother of the Muses, the prototype of the artist. As a rule, she selects and relieves out the important, omitting what is accidental or trivial. Now and then however, she makes mistakes like all other artists. Nevertheless, I take memory in the main as my guide."

My Life and Loves by Frank Harris

CHAPTER 1

How Shall I Begin?

Where shall I begin this tale of dozens of lovers and eight husbands? Too many men and too much sex, divorce, and heartache are the down-slant in this story. The up slant is a tale of love, romance, music, travel, happiness, fulfillment, and enjoyment. It has been difficult finding a place to start this true story and is why I came up with different openings. Should I begin with down-slant or up slant? For instance, here are a few openings I considered:

Opener #1 … I wonder, as many of you do, if we had our lives to do all over again, would we do it the same. Well, knowing what I know now, I would hope not. Although I do think I would have skipped marriage all together. It isn't due to what I've discovered in others, but of what I've learned about myself in the past decades.

Some of you have asked how I even remember the gazillions of relationships I've had? The answer to that is, one memory begats another, and then another, and there we go deeper into the memory pit.

Looking at it on the bright side, I feel maybe it all happened the way it did so I can share it with you, how about that? And maybe you and others can relate, going through what I went through, making the mistakes I did, thinking the way I did … and maybe just one of you might change your course and make better choices than I. I can only hope it wasn't all for naught.

Here's another beginning I planned:

Opener #2 … I am thrilled to be standing on the Promenade Deck of Cunard's largest ocean-liner Queen Mary 2 somewhere in the middle of the Atlantic Ocean, between Southampton, England and New York City. I recuperated from the seasick injection I received when I boarded. Waited till we left Southampton and were underway before going to my stateroom to nap, as the doc suggested. He said I'd acclimate in my sleep and wake as if I were on land. Magic! I did the same thing when I took a Seabourn cruise of four other seas, so I know that it works.

Tonight, I am dressed for dinner and out on the deck watching people, taking it all in. In four days, it will be my eightieth birthday. This is so exciting! A landmark birthday for me to celebrate on the QM2. The Bette Davis film - "Now, Voyager" - just crossed my mind while leaning against the ship's railing. As well as "Poseidon Adventure" and "Titanic."

But no matter what happens, sink or sail, it is such a gift to live this long, and such a gift I've given myself - this Cunard Atlantic Crossing. *Thank you, self! You are my best friend.*

As I look out at the moonlit sea of silver and black with glimpses of cobalt blue due to the ship's thousands of lights reflecting on the water, I think back through the years (I suppose eighty-year-olds reminisce at one time or another), and this night I have concluded that my entire life has been inundated and mostly consumed with men.

BUT … I had to chuck the QM2 opening because of the Corona Virus (Covid19) outbreak and had to cancel the Atlantic Crossing till the following year which would board seven months after my eightieth birthday. So, that one is of no use to me. Another time, another book.

And here's another option:

Opener #3 ... Yes, you read the title right, I've had eight husbands, although ten marriages if we count the two lucky ones I married twice. AND I've had dozens of lovers in between and sometimes during the marriages.

Now, please tell me all those relationships weren't an accomplishment of themselves ... I survived, didn't I? And did they not survive me to go on and marry others? I didn't spoil it for them, you might say I trained them for the next one. Or prepared them for what they didn't want. Yes, quite an accomplishment if you ask me. Could you do it? Happily? With no lingering bitterness? And take away what you've learned about yourself?

Admitted to your own shortcomings, not pointing a finger at the other person? Even if a few were assholes and I was a bitch, on occasion. But you won't hear name calling from me in this story. No, just the facts.

To set the record straight for a few uneducated, ill-intentioned gossipy spiteful persons, I loved all my husbands. Yes, I did. Or I would not have married them. I loved the lovers too, albeit some more than others. You see, one thing I've learned about myself is that I was in love with love. Loved them all at different levels, until I realized I didn't. In other words, I loved them at first. Some I had difficulty in loving past a point, or at any great length. And some you could say I was fond of, more than in love with them. But I *did not* ever marry for money!!! I dated men with money, but never considered them for marriage. Was and am a total romantic, and watch for it … I mistook infatuation for love. No surprise. There it is. I was confused and mistook the thrills and infatuation for soulmate love, *in all but one*. One was true love, which I didn't recognize at the time.

Oh, wait a minute, here's another possible beginning of the book, I decided not to use:

Starter #4 - I wonder if I would have married my teenage sweetheart Bert, would I have stayed married to him. We were engaged when I was a senior in high school, beautiful diamond ring and all. But because I was so afraid and ignorant of sex, the one night when he got too close to me and pushed his pelvis into mine on my front porch, and pinned me against the stucco wall, I couldn't breathe. We were fully clothed, of course. I was startled and confused at what I was feeling. My sudden desire mixed with panic, and his 'hard' desire, scared me. That was the first time he had

19

done that to me. Top half was okay, bottom half was taboo. I was so ignorant and naïve. I immediately shoved him away, thinking he wasn't respecting me, according to my mother who had warned me about boys continually. She warned they would try to get into my panties. Well, even though he didn't go for the panties, and never had, I threw the engagement ring at him and screamed, "It's over!" I ran inside the house. I am sure he was confused too. In hindsight, I admit I made a horrid mistake. I could've handled it wiser if I'd known better. But I didn't know.

When I finally did marry the first husband and went through months of adjusting to sex, yes months, I realized the serious blunder I had made with Bert. He was a normal, red-blooded, sexy 19-year-old young man. I wasn't normal. I was an uninformed, afraid, overprotected 17-year-old girl with no inkling or thoughts of sex and what marriage entailed. Totally unprepared. All I knew was that my friends were marrying, and I wanted it, too. You see, my strict upbringing shielded me from the normal boy-girl experience, sexual or otherwise.

Today, in all honesty, I would have preferred it be opposite.

Today, we are in a different world. Young girls are taught to use birth control pills if they must have sex as a teenager. And they have access to thorough sex education. In my day, there weren't any pills or education sources. There were 'rubbers" (prophylactics) and warnings.

I remember seeing a used rubber hanging on the handle of a front passenger side, quarter glass vent window. I couldn't figure out what it was. It looked disgusting. The car was parked by our high school tennis courts, and I knew the car belonged to an upperclassman, one of my classmates was going steady with him. So, they didn't notice when they threw it out the window the previous night, that it caught on the handle. That was the first time I saw a rubber. I was a junior in high school and the girlfriend with me told me what it was.

Now that I'm thinking, I was not only naïve, but I was also very sensitive in my early years … maybe over-sensitive to harshness, stern looks and hurtful words, misread actions. I remember I couldn't take friction or arguments of any degree. I would turn away, shut it out, or sometimes walk right out of the door and ofttimes out of the life of the boyfriend or out of the marriage. Didn't matter which. In the early days, maybe it was impatience on my part. I was very thin-skinned, felt every grimace, every raised eyebrow, took to heart every criticism - spoken or not, and as a result I began to build invisible protective shields around that tended to make me stronger and more determined, but more inward at the same time, shoving the feelings down deep. No wonder I now have elephant hide. It is very hard to wound me now. So, do not waste your time trying. I will just laugh and go on my way, shut you out, and close the imaginary walls tighter around me. I can reside perfectly well in that 3'x 3' shell. It's comfy and cozy.

My parents weren't critical of me though; at least I do not feel they were in any way responsible for my sensitivity. Some things we are born with, I truly believe. My dad was quietly controlling and made decisions for me. But he was a calm, not offensive, parental controller. I think that may have contributed to my rebellion when a man or anybody, as a matter of fact, tried to tell me how to think or what to do. Big mistake! Oh yes. Whopper of a mistake! The more men I married and the more lovers I had, the more I learned about myself. Consequently, I became more defensive and head strong. I couldn't stay long with any of them.

Women didn't play a major role in my life, but there were strong women around me, my aunts and grandmothers. However, no specific role models, I went off in a different direction than most. Sure, I admired a couple of my aunts who had talents in business and the arts, and a few teachers and writers as I got older. Would that be classified as role models? Probably. Anyway, I feel I am who I am, by my own doing. So, it is my own fault, can't put the blame on others. I feel good about that - what and who I am.

CHAPTER 2

Today and Yesteryear

A few more facts and then we'll get to the actual beginning of my story ...

My full maiden's name is Rebecca Joan McMullen, and I am writing this book. I include all the leading men in my life and what the effect of the diversified relationships had on me - emotionally, physically, and mentally.

Here are my married names in order: Isom Manos Brown Faeth Hein Clarkson Moore Buckley.

25

On my 80th birthday, September 7, 2020, I realized I was only twenty years shy of living a century. I've been a total of eight decades upon this earth (not counting my past lives)! Eighty was a pivotal birthday for me, and I know I've mentioned my age already, but I'm proud of it. It has been a momentous achievement for me. At least that's how I feel about it, surviving my life up to this point.

At the beginning of Year 2020, five years after my eighth husband died, and after selling my homes and business property in California, kit and caboodle, I began what was to be a year's adventurous journey abroad. Plans were to travel to different countries and stay the automatic visa limit (three or six months, depending on the country), then move on to another to stay the limit. Repeating the process over and over until I grew tired of traveling. Possibly continuing another year after that to parts unknown even beyond. I'd finally reached a time in my life of no responsibility other than to myself. A dream and goal of mine.

But my well-laid plan was suddenly cut short by Covid-19 shutting down borders between countries five months into my journey. I was still in England at the time, and I risked being there past the six-month limit on my UK visa while waiting and hoping the borders would reopen. Alas, I decided to return to the States, didn't want to risk becoming an illegal or prevented from returning to the US. Europe was already shutting down their borders, airlines and ground transportation was beginning to shut down too, which would impede my roaming the world as free as a wild bird.

I made last minute plans to settle in exciting Las Vegas on my return, making a new home in Nevada instead of returning to California. Thereby extending my adventure, not ending it.

I considered several towns and cities in the US where I might want to live, and finally made the best decision for my preferences, needs and requirements, and I am glad of it. I love it here in Las Vegas, love my beautiful cozy three-bedroom nest in a ten-story apartment building. It's a perfect, private, secure place to write my books without interruptions. The solitary living style I always wanted. It took me nearly six months to furnish and organize the space after I arrived, and to have my stuff delivered from storage in California.

As I lie here in my pink bedroom tonight (yes, pink fluff and lace, paintings of roses – comfy cozy), I am wondering how my life's journey ended up here, of all places. What lead me to this place and time? Why all the twists and turns and jumps through the hoops, springing from one male to the next, since a teenager, to finally land in Las Vegas at the ripe old age of 81? It truly makes me laugh. It does! I am not kidding. It is funny. Who would have 'thunk' it?

"Not I,' said the face in the mirror on the wall."

It does seem ironic, and you'll understand what I mean as I take you on this expedition through my men-relationships. But I must say upfront, all of it was meant to be. I am convinced I am exactly where I'm supposed to be, or I would not be here. I just took a crazy 'round-about way, and it took sixty-plus years of emotions, love and romances, tragedy and sadness, rock bottoms and heavenly peaks to reach my destination. Wait a minute … who's to say it is the last one? Ha ha. I may not be through yet.

It is amusing and amazing that when referencing a certain time-period or trying to remember when something in my past happened as I write this book, I think of the man I was with - husband or lover - to figure out the timeline.

For example, a question posed to me recently: *when did you work at Bozell Advertising on Wilshire Boulevard in Brentwood?*

Answer: *"Well, it came after the marriage to Larry, when the police came at midnight to protect me from him while I was packing the car to leave, then after the rescue by David Mac from a skid-row hotel in downtown L.A. before I went to Bull Head City to live with Jim H. who later was murdered."*

Yes, all true by the way – it is in Book Three of this series. And that describes how I figure timeframes – who, when, and where – giving me the year and the sequence. Not easy remembering so much in my crowded man-life.

So, last night I was reading one of my books about how to write a memoir, felt I needed some more technical advice. One of the exercises in the memoir how-to book suggested I state disappointments, list them and expound a bit. That should be easy to do, right? But it isn't.

I am still scanning my brain, searching for what may have been a disappointment. I don't think I've any in my vocational life; I always accomplished what I set out to do. I've a few regrets, like not pursuing a singing career or acting, but that isn't what is being asked, or is it? Am I disappointed about not becoming a professional singer or actor? No, I am not; got a taste of both along the way, glad I am who I am now. I am a writer, and very happy about it.

So, could my earliest disappointment have been the time my father wouldn't let me go to the Kern County Fair with Jerry S? You may laugh, but there it is … a male. I knew if anything, I could find a male in my past to illustrate disappointment. It has always been about men.

I was in high school. Jerry S had graduated when I was a freshman, we never dated but I had sort of a crush on him. Lots of secret crushes in high school. A couple years later, Jerry had come into the retail store where I worked and asked if I'd go to the County Fair with him that evening. I begged daddy to let me go, but he stood by another 'NO' decision, one of many. Remember, this was in the 1950s.

So, I stormed out of the stockroom door and went home from the five & dime daddy managed and where we all worked: my mother, two sisters and me. I hurried home in tears, hurt, and anger mixed with disappointment and embarrassment. Why wouldn't he let me go? I didn't understand why not, he didn't give a reason. I sped on, half running, it was about a 20-minute walk, as I recall. Was less at my pace that late afternoon. By the time I got home I'd worked myself up into such an emotional frenzy, feeling I had to make daddy sorry that he wouldn't let me go.

I knew where he kept his medications, in the cabinet over the refrigerator. I decided to take them all, every pill, and he would be sorry when I died from the overdose - such crazy, immature juvenile thoughts. I had no clue what the pills were, and I didn't care. All I thought was 'Boy, will he ever wish he had let me go'. It didn't enter my mind that my thinking was screwed up. But I'd worked myself into such a fray, I wasn't conscious of the reality of what I was doing, and the repercussions there would be, I just didn't care. I could have damaged my brain or liver permanently. (Hey, there's a big clue, Rebecca! Brain damage?) I could have become a bumbling fool instead of killing myself, dependent for the rest of my life, not going to fairs or anything with anybody. One never knows with pills, or any overuse, addiction, or attempt at suicide. But I hadn't learned yet.

A suicidal attempt could render a person totally incapacitated for life, a vegetable on life support. I've seen it with several people I've met over the years. And it never occurred to me that I'd be hurting my mother and sisters too, who had nothing to do with daddy's decision. Most of all, I hurt me. I was my own victim.

But obviously I wasn't in my right mind; I dumped the pills on the kitchen countertop and took them all, one by one, gagging and sobbing while a host of thoughts swirled in my head. I swallowed every single pill. Three containers. Like I said, I didn't know what the pills were. I had no idea at the time that in the future one of the major tragedies of my life would also be because of pills. Oh, if we could only foresee the future.

But at my young age of 16, I saw only the moment of disappointment. After taking all the pills, I put on my flannel pajamas my grandmother McMullen (Mamaw) had made, a Christmas gift, and I went to bed. It wasn't even dark yet. My plan was to go to sleep and not wake up. After a few minutes of waiting and nothing happening, I began tossing and turning, wondering when it would hit and how it would feel to die. I felt sick to my stomach. I got up and looked at the clock; the family was due to be home from the store. So, I went back to bed, covered my head with the quilt to hide the guilt that was surfacing. The reason for killing myself didn't seem as valid anymore, not so important. I was beginning to feel regretful and scared. And sick. Oh yes, very sick.

Then they arrived. I don't remember what sister Mary said when she saw me in bed, but she didn't know what was going on. Mary was a tomboy, no boyfriends yet. Wouldn't understand the hormones of a 16-year-old, I didn't either. Sister Martha was only six. Mother finally came in and told me to get up and eat supper (lunch was called dinner in those days).

35

But by then I was seeing double, then triple. Couldn't stand up. I fell sideways. I started crying, told mother what I did and said I was sorry that I'd taken all of daddy's pills. I was scared.

I don't remember what all happened next. I do remember Daddy was angry and he spanked me as I lay on the bed. Mother stopped him. Whether they called a doctor or not, the memory is gone, just isn't there.

I guess you could say I hadn't learned how to handle disappointment yet. And wouldn't you know it had to be over a guy, always because of a guy. Well, not so, it was because of me, my disappointment. Can't blame the poor fella for that. An innocent bystander, he never knew what had happened. No one did.

CHAPTER 3

The Beginning

I had my first orgasm when I was five years old, but I sure as hell didn't know what it was.

Now wait a minute, not to fear … it happened to me in first grade on the playground, alone on the monkey bars. Not orchestrated by some godforsaken, hell-bound, freaky pedophile.

Quite a coincidence that my mother called female genitalia a 'monkey', and for many years I couldn't say the word without thinking of my private parts instead of an animal at a zoo.

That first orgasm scared the living daylights out of me. It wasn't a full one; it was a slight erotic tingling wave that was triggered by the galvanized pipe monkey bars that I'd been straddling next to the lopsided merry-go-round on the playground. Being the tomboy that I was at that age, those days had been spent trying to learn how to maneuver the bars like the boys did. They hung by their knees, would swing and do a loop in the air and land on their feet. I wanted to do that. But when the tingling began that morning, I immediately jumped from the bar and darted guilty glances all around, looking for anybody that would have seen what had just happened. Nobody was looking.

I nervously smoothed out my little cotton dress Mamaw had made. In those days -1940s - little girls didn't wear jeans or peddle-pushers yet. My younger sister and I wore dresses, made from print cotton feed sacks by our grandmother. And when we hung by our knees on the bars, the dress skirts would fall over our faces, exposing little girl cotton panties and bare tummies.

That day, no one had paid any attention to the homely, drab little girl on the monkey bars. Drab would be me. I didn't know I was drab, but later in life I saw it in the photos of those times. I was drab. My dull brown hair, cut by mother wasn't kept well. It was straight and uneven, many times the crown hairs were gathered into a rubber band to keep out of my eyes. No adornment. Sometimes I wore a headband, which was different, or a scarf folded in a triangle. But I was not considered one of the pretty little girls in school.

I wonder, in my adult memories of that day, if I felt like a loner because of my shyness or how I felt about myself. I remember I felt alone, even around others. I always felt different, an oddball of sorts, and could play with paper dolls and later draw on rolls of shelf paper hours on end, not needing or wanting company or attention. My sister Mary was always not too far away, though. But that day the other children were preoccupied with what they were doing in their little groups on the playground. They weren't around me. Mary wasn't school age yet. So, little me was alone on the monkey bars.

You know, we all were not much more than toddlers in our first year of elementary school. And in my day, we played simple games on the school grounds at recess: we climbed the bars, there were balls to catch and throw, tether-ball poles, jump ropes, jacks, marbles, hop-scotch, the usual playground games of that era. I seem to recall a crude handmade merry-go-round and a teeter-totter. I know we had a teeter-totter at home my grandfather had built for us and our cousins. The schools offered very little then, compared to schools of today, but we were inventive. We didn't need much more. We climbed trees, ran, bicycled, jumped in mud puddles, wrestled, played tag, collected tadpoles, butterflies and what have you.

Nyeland Acres, where we lived, was a small community on California Hwy 101 between Camarillo and Ventura. A rural settlement of approximately 300 families who migrated from Oklahoma, Arkansas, Texas, Kansas, and other midwestern states. My grandfather Henry Allan Dearmore (Papa), who lived in his faded blue denim bib overalls, owned the grocery store on Nyeland Ave. We lived in the front house, across the driveway from the store. Papa and Mama lived in the house behind us, and there was another little house that Papa had built behind the store where my older cousin Helen lived with her blind husband and baby Linda.

Back to the orgasm: I was in a half stupor the remainder of the day, wondering what had happened to me on the monkey bars. What did I do to cause that feeling to come over me? And though

41

I tried and tried in the days to follow, I could never duplicate the feeling I'd experienced in those few moments. I must have been an absurd oddity before and after school each day, straddled atop that bar, squeezing my legs tightly around it in anticipation. I finally gave up. Whatever it had been, and whatever had caused it, was gone. It didn't matter. I soon forgot all about it.

And then it happened again, out of the blue, eight years later. One morning in my bed, in fact, an orgasm awakened me. I was thirteen and we lived in another part of California by then –1950s in a small farming town of Wasco in the San Joaquin Valley, northwest of Bakersfield. I woke up and it was happening again, but there was nothing causing it. No bars, no nothing. Totally confused and bewildered, I didn't move for what seemed like a very long time. I didn't want the feeling to go away. But it did. And still I knew nothing about my body and of course not about orgasms. I can call it an orgasm now, but back then I was clueless, and I sure as hell wasn't going to tell my mother or talk to anybody else about it. I hadn't even looked at that part of me. It was taboo!

"Do not look at each other down there!" my mother would say when my sister Mary and I'd take a bath together in the earlier years. "Do not touch yourself down there!"

But this time, in the privacy of my bed as a teenager, I touched myself where the sensation had happened, didn't look, only touched. Touching seemed to activate it again. Wha-!? I couldn't believe it! Long story short, that was the beginning of my lifetime of masturbation! So funny.

It was awkward at first, but it didn't take me long to learn how to manipulate myself to what I learned later was a clitoral orgasm. At the time, not knowing that I'd found my clitoris, and of course didn't know what the feeling was called, I didn't care. It felt good, and it was my secret.

I never told anybody, till now, about that experience. And I am mentioning it for two reasons: 1) I would hope all mothers will take kindly to and think about the possibility of early sexual awareness when your sweet baby reaches school age, 2) I believe this early occurrence for me was instrumental in my having an unusual, odd, secret sexual awareness early on and over the years.

So how did I go from that abrupt awakening to having eight husbands and many, many lovers? I ask myself now, after 80 years, did I know then, or for that matter have any inkling of what I wanted in life? Did I have dreams of marriage and raising children, or future goals or wishes, or overwhelming desires of accomplishment? Hell no! To all of it! I lived one day at a time – like we're told to do now. I don't remember having dreams of what I wanted to be when I grew up.

Sure, I loved to sing, draw, write, and play the piano. I certainly didn't think of choosing a career or a marriage, at thirteen. I was attracted to boys, and they to me, but I didn't think of sex, didn't know what it was. I didn't connect the dots. I didn't connect my masturbation with the opposite sex either. Why would I? That good feeling, I was beginning to crave, was all mine, I didn't even have fantasies in those early days, it was all about the feeling, only the feeling, while I was doing it.

I had much to learn, didn't I? One thing I do know, I evolved from the drab looking child to a not so bad looking teenage girl. I developed early, was wearing a bra at thirteen … bust 38, waist 22, hips 37, an hourglass figure. No fat. I still had problems with my hair though, permed frizzy, and couldn't decide on short or medium length. It embarrassed me most of the time, same as my feet. I wore size 8 shoes (9 now), while all the other girls wore 5, 6, or 7. I felt klutzy. So, the drabness had passed, now I had to deal with big feet and ugly hair. And the shoes my parents bought me were always a half size bigger. And they were white nurses' shoes. Can you imagine? Not the cute little saddle oxfords that everyone else wore. The nurses' shoes seemed to draw more attention to my feet. But I somehow got past that as I had with everything that bothered me by focusing on something else. And that something else was boys. Surprise, Surprise!

CHAPTER 4

Teen Loves

Paul B.

Bert B.

In my teens I had two loves that lasted for years – Paul and Bert. I'd classify both as first loves and they still occupy a prominent place in my heart today. I think of them often as I did through the years, special memories. They popped in and out of my life for decades after our teen romances in high school, even after I married and

47

divorced others. Both, Bert and Paul, married lovely brides and had daughters. Both have passed on, Paul several years ago, Bert recently.

I escaped having sex in my high school years with either of them or anybody else, as I mentioned before. And I fought petting like a trapped tiger. It led to sex and getting pregnant, my mother drilled into me, without telling me how and why. She didn't use the word sex; we didn't call it that in those days. She said 'intercourse', I abhorred that word of hers too. Anyway, I didn't know what intercourse or sex was, was told that 'bad' girls did it whatever "it" was, and however they did it.

It took Paul sixteen dates before I let him kiss me, he even 'bragged' to classmates about not kissing me on the dates. He counted the dates publicly as we went along. The bragging was not in a pompous, cruel brag sort of way, for he was always kind and loving. It was in a 'I-will-win-the-prize-eventually' kind of way, kidding about it. As if it were a game we were playing. I'd never been kissed by anybody before Paul. And of course, when it finally happened, I was in love – the start of a long career of my announcing "I am in love!"

I've always been romantic minded, from my preteen years when I learned and sang along all the love songs on 'Your Hit Parade', on the radio in the 1940s. My grandfather sold the hit parade magazines in his grocery store. I'd take one home with me every week and learn the lyrics of the latest hits, and I continued doing that when the show was televised from 1950 to 1959.

The black and white romance movies on TV in those early days would run one after the other on Saturdays – no sex or naked bodies of course. I'd sit and watch movies all day and be absorbed in them, dreamy-eyed. Began writing my own love stories when I was 10, using paper dolls and drawings at first - like storyboards on rolls of meat wrap paper from my grandpa's store and later rolls of white shelf-paper from my dad's five and dime.

Secret crushes on boys in elementary and junior high were before the ultimate dating in high school. My favorite eighth grade crush was Monte B. He was so handsome. Still is, in his eighties.

I need to clear up a few things before I go any further. I was never a sex addict, as a few have asked. To me, marrying so many times and having dozens of lovers was never based on sex, as difficult as that is to believe. Flies to flypaper, which was once told to me. Me being the flypaper. I didn't seek out boys and men. They just appeared.

Never being crazy about sex, I suppose I was a good actress in later years. I never felt the female and male genitalia were attractive. The rest of the body-parts were okay, just not the penis and vagina – there, I've said it! Two more words I've always disliked with a passion. The craziest thing about this is, I probably ended up having more sex than all my gal pals put together. Not on purpose, just happened that way.

When it finally happened, I became quite the expert at hiding my true feelings during sex, which most likely began when my mother told me on before my first wedding night, "A man must have intercourse, it's their nature. It's your duty as his wife. So just lie there and think of something else, and pretend you like it. You won't like it."

On looking back, that told me a lot about mother, and explains the lack of physical affection shown between my parents in our house growing up. Oh, they loved us, no question about that, they just didn't smooch on each other or us – no kisses, hugs, touching. This is my memory; my sisters may remember it differently. Daddy did love on sister Martha though. He adored her when she was

RJ Buckley

a child. We all did. She was a cutie, and comical too. She always made us laugh, still does today at 70.

So, I did what my mother told me with Jim (husband #1) when we finally had sex. Not on our wedding night though. As it turned out, I had to be cut before he could penetrate. How embarrassing! Proof I didn't have sex before marriage, People!!! Ha! I know everybody thought that Paul or Bert got to me in high school. Nope, I was a virgin till months after I was married. But on top of everything else, surgery - which has always terrified me, made the thought of sex even more scary and unattractive.

But wait, I am getting ahead of myself here. I'm writing about my teen loves in high school in this chapter …

PAUL B.

I noticed Paul when I was a freshman in high school, he was a junior. I was attracted to him at first because of his handsome flirtatious looks, his laugh, and his deep singing voice. I loved his basso vocals. To die for. Music and singing was dear to me, so I lived that desire vicariously through him. Oh yes, I admit it, I adored Paul for his talent and his good looks, and how he treated me. He sang all over the county in churches and at events and won talent contests. I was proud to be associated with him.

We first began talking when I was a sophomore in typing class, he was a senior. He sat across from me. I adored him from the get-go, didn't matter to me that his legs were paralyzed, and he wore braces due to the Polio he contracted in eighth grade. It didn't bother me at all that he swung himself from the hips on wooden crutches to get around. I can honestly say I never noticed it; I was totally mesmerized and hooked by his personality. I loved everything about Paul. His hair was wavy, well-trimmed and in place, except for the wayward curls that would sometimes fall on his forehead. I loved his aroma too; it was of horehound candy – those little hard old-fashioned brown candy drops. He kept a supply in his car and shirt pocket, and he would continually suck on them like a cough drop to assure his throat and vocal cords were well lubricated for rehearsals and performances. I can still smell him. For many years in my adult life, married or not, I would maintain a supply of horehound candies in a candy dish, reliving the aroma of Paul I so loved. I have a vintage glass candy dish, with lid, specifically for them now, sixty-five years later. I just popped one into my mouth, the only sweet I will have today. Watching my weight.

On our sixteenth date we had our first kiss. I didn't know what to expect, how it would feel. I remember his kisses were wet and loose. I had puckered for the event and his lips engulfed mine completely. I was so embarrassed. I didn't think it would be like that. I knew I was doing something wrong. So, it was awkward for me, and I am sure it was for him. We didn't talk about it. Needless to say I quickly adapted to his method of kissing.

All those dates when I first battled his necking attempts, I also fought his hands from roaming under my skirt and the layers of crinoline slips. He just wanted to touch my legs, he said, as I pushed and pulled his hands from under the yards of fabric that served as an unplanned safeguard of my virginity - although I didn't know what that was in those days. But lordy, he was determined! He would ask me what color panties I was wearing each day, just to agitate me, while we sat together in study hall. A teaser, he was. I was fond of his laugh when he would deliberately try to shock me with the things he'd say. If my parents would have known what was going on, they would surely have sent me to an all-girls school, like they threatened a time or two. But we were innocently playful, nothing more.

After school, Paul would drive us to Jack's drive in or the Slush Pit for cokes where we would hang out with other kids, then he'd drive to the baled haystacks at the edge of town on the highway, or to some other obscure spot to 'neck'. Although I resisted him, I looked forward to those times. I liked being held by his warm, strong arms. And I really wanted to kiss him from the first, but because I didn't know how, that alone kept me from it. One reason being, I was self-conscious about not knowing. I'd practice on my arm when I lay in bed at night, but my arm couldn't be how a kiss felt, a flat nothing. That prolonged my withholding more than anything else. Another reason was mother's incessant warnings about kissing. So, after our attempt sessions, he'd drop me off to work at the five & dime. Another kiss-less day would end. 16 dates of no lip locking. Ridiculous.

It's worth repeating, I was so proud to be Paul's girlfriend. There were a few girls that didn't like it, though. Especially the Mennonite girls in our school. Paul was a Mennonite. Anyway, whatever their reasons, I haven't a clue. But they were downright rude to me. I was always happy about other teen couples being an item, no resentment whatsoever, no jealousy, just thought how lucky they were to be together. So, disapproval from his gal pals was a mystery, and hurtful to me.

By the way, for those wondering, I easily adapted to his way of kissing.

We continued to date that year and through the summer till he went away to college in the fall and out of sight out of mind became a reality. But we weren't over yet.

BERT B.

I really don't remember how Bert and I got together. We saw each other every day on the high school campus and at football games, he, being a player, me, a yell & song leader a couple of seasons. We didn't have any classes together; he was a year ahead of me, so we only saw each other in passing. I think it finally began with him asking if I'd like to go to Jack's Drive-In after school for a coke. Eventually those casual dates would end with quick make-out sessions – only kisses. I had to relearn how to pucker, for that was Bert's way. I was nervous at our first attempt, for I felt it was like when I first kissed Paul, only it was reversed. I was Paul, Bert was me. I adjusted soon enough. Everybody kisses differently, I found out.

Then he asked if he could drive me home after a game. Those two events became our regular dating pattern. But to pick me up at home to go somewhere else, that was another story. My parents didn't know him, and they questioned whether he went to church and was a Christian. Oh boy. I started worrying they wouldn't let me be with him, and I liked him very much and was feeling it was more than that.

His eyes twinkled, and he was always grinning and flexing his muscles at me. I smile still, when I think about him. Bert was a very sports-minded fella, did it all. Worked with his brothers at the family lumber yard. So, he was well-built physically as well as emotionally and mentally healthy.

I loved the way he spoke in short, clipped sentences. Three-word sentences. "I be me." "I be Bert." "I be waiting." I've run across some lyrics and poetry that always remind me of his playful short sentences. He would be like a child, just learning how to put together sentences. Like the See Jane Run primary books. He would always grin with laughing eyes. Never changed over the years, always the same.

"Do you go to church? Are you a Christian? I'm asking because my parents want to know."

He answered, "I'll go to church with you, if you want me to. Will that make them happy?"

"Very happy." I hugged him.

After that, he would join me for church on Sunday mornings, every Sunday. That seemed to quell the notions of mother and daddy not letting me date him. Success!

We were allowed to have dates related to school and church, but nothing else. That encompassed school sports at home and away, school field trips, church field trips, and church camp. And we continued our after-school trysts: cokes at Jack's or the Slush Pit and quick rides in the country before I had to be at work in daddy's store. The quick rides to the country were kissing sessions, and of course his futile attempts at petting, much more determined than Paul, however. Another red-blooded, sexual teen-aged boy. Poor Bert. I was able to fend him off, but to exhaustion.

However, Bert driving to church camp near Yosemite that summer, changed everything. I sat close to him while he drove, his left hand on the steering wheel, his right arm across my shoulder and his hand dangling. At one point he touched my breast, grazed the nipple. OMG! I felt it through the blouse and bra. It tingled to my soul and back. My goodness! I'd never felt that before. That was the beginning of his fondling my breasts. Bert, as well as me.

Remember, I already masturbated in the privacy of my bed at night, and sometimes the restroom of my dad's store during the day.

Surprise, surprise! Yep, tis true. But I still didn't connect the dots. Masturbation was my own, didn't have anything to do with a boy. And now his touching my boobs gave me something to add to the equation. It worked for me, by myself, and the imagery began. I'd imagine Bert touching my breasts while I masturbated, I would close my eyes and touch my own nipples. Let me tell you, that was a dynamic process I'd discovered. But I didn't tell Bert. However, from then on, he could feel my "boobies" (that's what he called them) anytime he wanted – in the car, in movies, at sports games under the blanket … I laugh when I think back that I thought no one knew what was going on under the blanket. They had to notice at one time or another – my glassy eyes, movement under the blanket at breast level, flushed face. Surely.

We dated regularly, were going steady, as it was called in those days. After a few months he asked me to marry him. I don't recall the actual moment in time, but I said yes. I didn't want to be without him. He was natural and comfortable. And I loved his family: his parents, his three brothers and three sisters. I don't remember seeing his oldest sister much, I think she was already married and had moved to the northwest. The two oldest were married, I believe. My family loved Bert too, even my Aunt Mable, the decorator, mother's sister. Those added to my reasons to marry him. No conflicts.

I remember one Sunday afternoon we rode by his brother's house, he and his brother lived there I believe, memory has waned. I think they designed and built the house together. There were a lot of cars parked around it. Cars I recognized.

"What's going on there today?" I asked.

"Looks like a party. You want to stop a minute? I'll show you the fur pillows your aunt Mabel gave me."

I said, "Okay," and we went in.

And we left a quick couple minutes later, for it was a gangbang party. I will leave it at that. Whether he knew about it or not, it is unimportant to me now. He explained what a gangbang was after we left. Said an older woman had been paid to come there to "entertain" the boys, one by one. I'd never heard of such a thing, and he apologized for taking me in. I didn't understand what they were doing. Drinking beer and taking turns to go into the bedroom? As it turned out, he was furious that they were using his fur pillows for props under the woman. Not a good thing all the way around.

So, our teenage life went on, I adored Bert, we were a twosome, engaged to be married. Our occasional evenings and Sundays together were special, until the night I mentioned earlier in this book, when he pressed too close to me on my front porch, and I panicked. I threw the ring at him and said we were through. That was the most asinine thing I could have done, and I realize that wholeheartedly now. I hurt him in the moment and regretted it for years afterwards.

We both went on to marry someone else, he a few years later than me. He didn't marry till I left my first husband.

RETURN TO PAUL B.

I was 17 the summer after I graduated high school in 1958, four months after I'd thrown the engagement ring at an unfortunate unsuspecting Bert, I reconnected with Paul. He was home from Westmont College for the summer working as a disc jockey at KWSO the local radio station, as he did every summer. My plans were to go to Ventura Junior College in the fall, I was already enrolled.

One night, after an emotional episode at home, l ran away and ended up hiding all night in Paul's car, parked in one of the farm garages at his house. Paul's father was a cotton and potato farmer

65

in the San Joaquin Valley – Wasco/Shafter area. I wound up that night in Paul's car. He didn't know I was there, no way to call him, no cell phones then. I watched the family through the windows as they ate dinner and eventually went to bed. Lights were off. I went to his car, lay on the back seat in the dark, in shorts and T-shirt, afraid and crying. Didn't know what to do. I felt just like I did over the Jerry S. and county fair debacle. Same as I did at the very moment, I realized I shouldn't have taken daddy's pills. One might say I was impulsive, you think?

I'll back up here and explain how I got to this point.

It had started out as another ordinary Sunday, except mother and daddy had decided to drive three hours south to Oxnard to visit the McMullen clan for the day. We three sisters (17, 16, 8) wanted to stay home, it was summer and our only day off from working six days at daddy's store.

I think Mary may have gone off with one of her girlfriends and Martha was playing in the backyard most likely. I probably was playing the piano and singing, going from cover to cover through songbooks and hymnals, which was my favorite pastime.

Paul telephoned and asked if he could come over to see me. I said yes, excitedly. That afternoon we talked about his college in Santa Barbara, about my plans to go to Ventura in the fall, and even touched on a possible future together after college. That surprised me. I didn't know what I'd be doing in a year, much less in two years. And I never felt like his parents approved of me, as Bert's did. So, I just passed right over that topic. It was fun visiting that afternoon, no smooching at all. I fixed some sandwiches for us, it was nearing early evening, but not dark yet. We all ate and then Paul, on his crutches, leaning against the sink counter, helped me do dishes.

That's what we were doing when my folks returned. They were both stunned to see Paul there and upset that he was. Daddy ordered him out of the house, while I stood dumbfounded and confused. On Paul's way to the front door, I followed and said I was sorry to him. But daddy wasn't through yet. I don't remember all that was said, but what stuck in my mind was, "You can't even have children, so you can't marry her. Don't come around Becky anymore!"

We must've said in defense earlier, that we were talking about marriage. I don't remember. But for daddy to have said that, most likely we did. I was mortified! You can imagine how Paul felt. I was crying, Paul was hurrying out the door on his crutches.

After he was gone my dad took off his belt and tried to lash out at my bottom, but I'm no dummy, I sat in a chair, hoping to deter him. Things got completely out of control. Mother was screaming at him to stop, for he'd started using his belt on my legs. Martha jumped on his back, crying … it was a horrid few minutes. I refused to cry, to react in any way. I finally got up and went to my bedroom, shut the door, crawled out the window, and ran away. To where, I didn't know. I just wanted to get away from all that turmoil.

So, a few hours later, in the darkness, here I was in Paul's car in his dad's garage. I worried about what Paul would say at 4:30 a.m. when he would come out to drive to the radio station. I was worried about the dirt and mud on my clothing – shorts and top. My thighs with red marks and dried blood traces where daddy's metal belt tip (?) had accidentally struck in fury - and my bare feet dirtying the pristine tuck & roll leather seat covers. I was worried about the menstrual odor coming from an overloaded Kotex pad. I was a complete mess. A 17-year-old high school graduate run-away. Ridiculous!

Paul loved his 1949/50(?) Ford with the Continental Kit, and rightfully so, for it was his mode of transportation that was more important to him than most others our ages. His car was rigged so that he could accelerate and brake with his hands, since he couldn't use his legs and feet. Polio did that to him. He was two years older than me, and I thought I loved him. I'd forgotten all about Bert.

As I lay there, waiting, I worried about what would happen to me when and if I went home. If I went home? But where else would I go? I'd have to go home. Didn't want to think about that.

The distance to the farm from town where I lived was several miles. I don't know how many exactly, I don't remember. And I wasn't entirely sure how to get to his house in the first place. I zigzagged over the irrigated farmland, the route I'd chosen was through the fields rather than taking the roads, in case someone was looking for me. I would lie flat on the dirt every time I saw headlights. A bit dramatic, I agree.

But I made it to the farm, don't know how, but I did.

When he opened the car door, he exclaimed, "Mack!" His nickname for me.

"I am so sorry; I've been here all night and I smell bad and must look awful. I'm sorry. But I didn't know where else to go."

He told me to get in the front seat and tell him about it on the way to the radio station. I did. And we decided after his early morning show, he would take me to his married sister's house where I could shower and clean up. That's what we did.

Although, I cleaned up somewhat in the restroom at the radio station. Rinsed out my panties and made a paper towel sanitary napkin.

71

The damp panties held the folded paper towels in place well enough.

I really liked his sister and her husband, they had a paint store in town, not far from the five & dime. And she was always kind to me. I think I stayed there the next night too, and finally phoned mother.

Long story short … my uncle Bill had arrived later that week, and mother suggested I return to Oxnard with him, stay with my grandmother for a while, then decide what was next. So off to grandmother's house we went, and I was there the rest of the summer.

In the meantime, Paul went to a doctor and got a letter stating there was nothing wrong with his ability to have children.

He gave the letter to my father.

But I was in Oxnard then, and that summer I met my first husband to be.

CHAPTER 5

Other Lovers

Several "Other Lovers" repeatedly appeared off and on in my life over the years, including Bert and Paul, and others you haven't met yet. You see, I remained long-term friends and sometimes intimate with those I loved but didn't marry. However, I wasn't intimate with Paul, other than kissing, even though we met several times through the years; I even published three of his books when I was a publisher in Arizona. Such a talent he was, not only in music, but as an author and painter.

Loved him till the very end. And I felt close to him all those years. Even around his wife and daughter, I wasn't interfering or taking away from their love relationship.

I guess I still needed a connection with him. Maybe I felt guilty the way it turned out that summer before I married someone else. My parents' attitude, my change of feelings. I felt bad, there was a lot of guilt there. I responded to every phone call from him in the years that followed, wrote letters, and edited and published his books at no cost to him, my gifts. I even pitched in and helped by being one of the vocals on one of his recordings, although I wasn't qualified. That was his doing. He talked me into it. I was always glad to see him though, so that had something to do with it. He was a dear, dear friend always, and I felt the same from him. He never missed sending me a card at Christmas and on my birthday.

But obviously, I quickly learned I wasn't cut out to be monogamous. I must've had some male middle eastern genes going on in my past life psyche, for I could have been happy with a harem. Not being in a harem, having one. A male harem. And then again, if I would have married all my loves, their times in my life would've been cut short. Marriage seemed to be the abrupt end, the beheading of my relationships - am thinking of my male counterpart, King Henry the Eighth, at the moment.

Another who lingered for quite a few years in my mind and heart was David Mac, a sax player, who I met while I was temping at the Foundation for the Junior Blind in Los Angeles. Dearest David's day job was as a music teacher for the blind. I worked in the office, assistant to the executive director. As soon as personnel got wind that David and I were an item, I was asked to move it on down the road. Fraternizing was against the rules. But we continued to see each other in the next few years, off and on. He's another one I didn't marry, although he did ask me to marry him in an alcohol moment. Ha! He is in the 'Other Lovers' category, one of my favorites, by the way. It turned out right, for I wouldn't have been good for him. I am eighty now, he's sixty-three. OMG! Talk about a puma, or cougar. Either. But I was in love with David, regardless. He is in Book Three's timeframe. I don't think there are any other lovers than these that lasted for years.

Oh my God! I almost forgot Jim A. Now there was an off and on romance that stretched over twenty-five years! How could I forget him? He was married, lived in Seattle at first, represented well-known brands in clothing manufacturing, traveled a lot. I first met him in San Francisco on a business trip, both of us there on business, and I fell smack dab in love & lust. That story in a later volume too. And mustn't forget Cal T. and Alex M., both I met at the

Madonna Inn in SLO (Book Two). Several other

lovers have passed, too. I am outliving them all …

I WIN. What do I win, you ask? I win some

wonderful memories and an extraordinary life.

CHAPTER 6

Descriptions: Who & What?

I will answer that question here in chronological paragraphs ... I feel I've already said enough to give you a hint of my before-marriage years, the family dynamics I experienced. And I touched on my teen 'loves' and a few of my long-term affairs which I will get into later.

First, I must say, after watching Elizabeth Taylor's biopic series, that her reasons for her seven husbands were more for a neediness of love than mine were. She needed the deep immersion of loving and being loved, to the point of suffocation and possession, love addiction, if you will. Her alcohol and pill dependence were addictions too. I was in love with love, yes. And I was drawn to the ecstatic, giddy, heady feeling of infatuation that inevitably led me to saying the binding three little words that carried so much weight with a man. With me, many of the male relationships were short-lived, however. If they made it past three months, there might be somewhat of a commitment or attachment on my part. But most didn't last past a few dates. And the fellas were confused by my sudden break offs and excuses.

Julie London described my young, naïve approach best on one her recordings, a favorite that I listen to quite often:

"If I expected love when first we kissed,
Blame it on my youth.

If only for you I did exist

Blame it on my youth ...

I believed in everything,

Like a child of three.

You meant more than anything,

All the world to me!"

BUT I WILL STATE THIS FACT ...

I fell in love and married; I fell out of love and divorced. I have no regrets for marrying who I married and divorced.

Here's a brief description of the eight men I married ... all have passed on, so I am the last word on our courtships, relationships and marriages. I survived them. The pages in these books are MY memories:

1. JIM I: An 18-year-old just like me when we married. We met the summer after we graduated at my cousin's party in the Oxnard area. He joined the Army after our engagement in the fall, attended college after the Army, obtained a master's degree. Retired as the Social Services Director of Ventura County of California. A very pleasant and kind person, always. Father of my first son. Married four years. Jim is deceased.

2. MITCH M: A 28-year-old, I was 25, when we married. He did a stint in the Air Force in Korea. When we met at Oxnard Bank of America, he was a computer technician for civilian Federal Electric Corp, contracted to NASA. He was on the ship RANGE TRACKER based in Port Hueneme. His job was to

track Gemini Missiles over the Pacific
after being shot from Vandenberg AFB.
He was promoted off ships to the Human
Resources Department at Vandenberg as
a recruiter. Later he retired and opened
his own employment office to man
technical positions. His father died when
he was three, didn't know his mother,
lived in children's homes and foster
homes till he was 16 when he lied about
his age and joined the USAF. He had a
dark side (do not we all?). Married nine
years, we had two sons. Mitch is
deceased.

3. GARY B: A 37-year-old, I was 34 when
   we married a couple months after we met
   at Cambria Pines Lodge at a Billy Mize
   concert. He had been in business with his
   father as a plumber but was a Hearst

Ranch cowboy when we met. Also
sought after as one of best at shoeing
horses, and he tended bar for extra
income. He was a big man, a gentle giant
most times, unless provoked, which I
discovered firsthand. He abhorred cities
and crowds of strangers and didn't travel
more than a couple hours from home.
After retiring from cowboying, he was
hired by the State of California as head
of plumbing at the historical Hearst
Castle at San Simeon. We were married
three and a half years. Gary is deceased.

4. JERRY F: We married twice – First
   time, he was 45 years old, I was 38.
   Second time, two years later. Holder of a
   master's degree he was Chief of
   Detectives of San Luis Obispo Sheriff's
   Department when we met. Commander

of SWAT. A fun-loving jokester on his off time. Retired, became assistant director of security of AAA Los Angeles Headquarters. Then the shit hit the fan. Married three years total. Jerry is deceased.

5. CHARLEY H: 50 years old, I was 48 when we married. With Stanford BS and MBA degrees, Charley was working for a conglomerate of corporations to oversee/manage grape vineyards, orange and lemon groves in Kings Canyon, Tulare, and Kern Counties. He was based in Visalia. Total alcoholic … I found out too late, for we married after our fourth date. Fun-loving guy, until he wasn't, and I wasn't. Marriage lasted three months, two of them he was in Rehab. Charley is deceased.

6.   LARRY C: Don't remember his age, I think he was two or three years older than me. I was 49, almost 50. Larry had been a Green Beret and later was contracted as a mercenary to Central and South America. He retired to San Bernardino County in construction. Built houses. We were married in Mexico, lasted one year, didn't end well. Scary! I believe he's deceased.

7.   PHILIP M. 60 years old, I was 57 when we married in Oundle, England. Philip was an automotive engineer early on before I knew him, when we met was CEO of his own corporation that processed green waste into viable products. He was an environmentalist. Went all over the world pitching his

85

patented process. A' cheerio' fellow, except for his occasional business tantrums and his questionable financial methods and dealings. We had an unusual marriage arrangement, but we remained friends over the years, even though our marital relationship ended early on. Philip is deceased.

8. JIM B: My eighth and last husband. He was 89 when we married, I was 61. Twenty-eight years apart, a big gap. He was a retired window dresser of major department stores in New York City and Beverly Hills, and a display/interior designer in Los Angeles, also a television show set designer. His final retirement took him to Cambria, California to live where he first delved into real estate, buying and selling, and then opened his

own community theatre – The Pewter Plough Playhouse. We were married in Las Vegas, Nevada in Sept 2001 twelve days after the attack-and-destroy of the Twin Towers in New York City. Jim was ultra-artistic, egotistical to the extreme (rightfully so, he earned it), a very smart and talented man. And although we had much in common, we couldn't live together, separated after four years. The true story is in the fourth volume of these writings. But we were together again the last year of his life, after his son died. Jim is deceased.

So, there you have it … and now on with the story … ***Husband Number One***.

Still in my teens, however – both of us 18.

CHAPTER 7

Husband Number One

JIM I.

Just a mention, I've had several Jims, they weave in and out of my man life, as you'll see. My elementary school first crush was a James, called J.C. He was my favorite until I was ten years old when we moved upstate.

Then in high school a crush on Jim P. when I was a senior. He was the one date wonder to see "The Ten Commandments" at the Fox Theatre in Bakersfield. Then he was off to marry his fiancé a few weeks later, a shock to me, didn't know he was engaged. Why the hell did he ask me out on a date that summer? Like everybody else, he probably thought I was easy. Showed him, though, didn't I? Ha!

Then came my first husband, Jim I. - the first Jim husband. The second Jim spouse, was the last husband. Bookends. And other Jims in-between.

To reiterate, before I was eighteen, I had broken up with two high school serious sweethearts, and left Wasco to get away and spend the summer in Oxnard primarily to separate from my parents for a while. Emotions had been high and hurtful after the broken engagement to Bert B., and the Paul B. fiasco. So, I stayed with my Grandma Besse (Mamaw) and my Uncle Bill for the summer. They lived together.

I loved it at my grandma's. Who doesn't love their grandmothers? And Uncle Bill made me laugh all the time. He was good for me. I adored him. His stories of work at the Camarillo Mental Hospital kept me in stitches. And I enjoyed all my McMullen cousins and aunts and other uncles too. AND the Dearmore side of the family, my mother's brother, Uncle Bob, and two of their other sisters, Aunt Mable and Aunt Edith, lived in Ventura County at that time too, so they were fun to visit. A lot of relatives on both sides.

Cousin Sally was Uncle Bob and Aunt Elva's daughter. Sally called me and invited me to a house party at their ranch in Somis-Camarillo area. I always loved to go there. Aunt Elva was a social butterfly and made me feel so welcome. I felt like Uncle Bob preferred my sister Mary over me. So, I leaned towards Aunt Elva. Anyway, I went to the party and there were girls and boys of high school age, and recent graduates of Oxnard

High that lived in Camarillo. I was introduced to Jim I. at that party. He was there with his buddies – Neal, Howard, and Cervando.

Jim and I talked a lot, and I was amused how much he reminded me of Jim P. from Wasco, who I'd had a crush on. The fellas even had the same first and middle names – James Edward. Later I compared their HS senior photos, and it was uncanny how much they looked alike. That may have had something to do with my initial attraction to Jim I., the other attraction was that he wasn't eager to touch or kiss me, was a gentleman and a nice guy. It was easy to be with him. I had just come from a very physical relationship with Bert, remember, and a disturbing union with Paul. So, Jim and I easily became friends, we dated, no touchy-touchy feely-feely. It was a welcome relief. If we kissed, I do not recall, but it must have been light, not make-out heavy-duty. Surely, we must have kissed, but I can't remember. A good night peck, if anything. I just do not remember other than that. So, because of the contrast, I must have felt Jim was the one. I felt that he respected me, just as mother said, because he didn't get physical. So of course, when he asked me to marry him that summer, I said yes! Of course! All my friends were getting married too. I was very fond of him by then.

Jim joined the Army with his buddies when we were engaged, with the plan to get married after boot camp, before his advance parachute training back east. I drove to Monterey CA almost every Sunday to visit him during Army basic training. We usually spent the day in Carmel or Monterey or visited my cousin Jerry Sanford who was living off base with his wife Louise. He was at Fort Ord too, at the same time. And my other 'cousin' Jo Mattis, who lived in Monterey with her handsome Portuguese fisherman husband Frank, and their beautiful little daughter Debbie. I loved

visiting Jo. It is because of her, still to this day, I

use an over the door shoe rack. Gives me a cozy,

homey feeling. I loved looking at her fancy, glitzy

spike heels. She loved to dance. Jo wasn't really

my cousin but was connected to my Aunt Iva

(mother's sister) in some way. As a girl she spent a

lot of time with my aunt. Anyway, I loved driving

to Monterey for the day and visiting my cousins, as

well as my teenage husband to be.

But I had second thoughts about Jim even

then. One such time was while he was at Fort Ord

in basic training, the movie makers came to Kern

County, outside our little farm town of Wasco. I

was living back home then, waiting to be married.

They were to film a crop-duster airplane scene

over a cornfield with Cary Grant running through

the fake cornfield. My girlfriend and I went out

there one day to watch the filming, she knew Cary

Grant's double and wanted to see him. (I wrote a short story about this experience in one of my short story collection books "Love has a Price Tag".)

So, here I was … eighteen years old with the voluptuous body of a woman and the maturity of a green pea. Since the age of thirteen, I'd been self-conscious of an oversize bosom, tiny waist and curvaceous hips; I cringed when boys and men looked at me with their overload of testosterone, staring at my body parts instead of my eyes. This was the age of Marilyn Monroe, Jayne Mansfield and Sofia Loren - the mid '50s, when curvy women were popular same as they were in the Rubenesque era, and for the same reasons. Most girls would die for body-look-alikes of the shapely movie stars. But not me. I wanted to be tall and slim, not as I was.

Normally I wore clothing that hid my embarrassing physical attributes, but that day I had decided to wear a low neck, fitted bodice, pink corduroy dress that Mrs. Correll had sewn for me. She made some of my clothes, except for the ones I ventured to make and the winter wool pleated skirts and fashionable lamb's wool and angora sweaters. Winter stuff was purchased at Keith's Apparel, next door to the five & dime. But the fabric for all the rest of my clothing came from our store. My mother would select the yardage and choose the patterns and take a regular supply to Mrs. Correll who'd charge minimal to make a dress. But like I said, sometimes I made my own, learned how to sew in junior high on a Singer treadle machine.

Although it had been a hot month of August in the San Joaquin Valley, summer temperatures always in the three digits, I selected the corduroy to wear because I wanted to wear my new pink patent leather shoes and that was the only pink dress I owned. I had a striped, lavender and purple denim dress, but the pink shoes clashed with it. So, despite

95

the warm weather, I wore the winter corduroy to work. But it was at least a summer pastel color. The four crinoline slips warmed it up even more and lifted the skirt making it appear as if I was a ballerina in mid-calf length puffiness. I wore a pink headband in my short, curly, auburn hair and thought it completed the pale pink ensemble very nicely.

My girlfriend, Lynn, was going to pick me up at work on my lunch hour in her new white Triumph sports car that was a birthday present (I think), and then we were going to drive out to the site of the filming of "North by Northwest". Only a few minutes before Lynn was to arrive, I asked my dad if I could have a two-hour lunch so I could go watch a film crew make a movie outside of town.

"I don't see any point in that," he said to me. "What good will it do to go watch a film crew making a movie? Those people are different than us."

"I know that Daddy. But Lynn wants me to go with her; she doesn't want to go out there by herself. We'll be all right. We'll stick together. She knows one of the doubles. She went to riding school with him. Please, Daddy. Let me go?"

"It's against my better judgment, but alright. And if you're not back in two hours, I'll come looking for you."

And I knew he would. He'd done it before. As I stood in front of the store waiting for Lynn, I wondered if daddy would still be as overprotective when I was married. I looked down at the tiny diamond on my finger. The ring Bert had given me was prettier with bigger diamonds. At that moment I didn't know exactly how I felt about being engaged, even though it seemed like the thing to do.

I didn't want to go to college like my dad wanted me to do. I was tired of school. And I didn't want to live at home anymore. So, there was nothing else I could do. Or so, I thought.

Lynn honked the horn, disturbing my depressing reverie.

The film company had leased a few acres of land out in the middle of nowhere and had hired students from our high school to build fields of corn for them – sheets of plywood with holes drilled and corn stalks stuck in the holes, forming rows of corn. They built a beautiful, portable cornfield and transported it 25 miles west of our town, to the alkaline, arid fields of tumbleweed, where no decent crops would grow then. Now it's an agricultural Mecca.

It was the third day of filming. Lynn was excited about seeing her riding mate again. She loved horses and had learned to ride English style and to jump horses at a riding academy in the San Fernando Valley near Los Angeles where she'd met George. I'll call him George; I don't remember his name. He was older than Lynn's 18 years (we shared the same birthday, by the way), but nonetheless they had corresponded and kept in touch. And it just so happened he was Cary Grant's double. This was a Cary Grant movie - "North by Northwest."

Lynn turned the car off the two-lane highway 446 (in those days) past Lost Hills onto the well-worn semi-paved road that led to where all the crew trucks and trailers were parked. It looked like the entire town had driven out to the site. The vehicles bordered the contrived corn field. If you didn't know any better, you would have thought it was a real field. Our WUHS shop class outdid itself.

They were filming the scene of the crop-dusting plane swooping down into the corn field while Cary Grant was hiding among the stalks, trying to escape the villains. Only it wasn't Cary Grant, it was his double. Cary Grant wasn't there. I figured they wouldn't subject a star of his caliber to that sweltering heat, anyway. They were doing long shots and shots not showing the face, for which they used the double.

We stood on the sidelines watching as shot after shot was filmed. We were told that the next day they were shooting a plane crash, where the crop duster hits a car, a rural couple is driving.

"I wish we could come out and see that, too," I whispered to Lynn. "But no way will Daddy let me come out here again. In fact, look at the time. We need to be going back."

"Okay, I just want to talk to George on his break. I've got to at least say hi to him, I told him I'd be here."

"All right. I'll just go on back to the car and wait. But hurry." I was bored and it was too hot to stand there watching takes and retakes. Movie making is such a slow process.

I took a deep breath of the hot air and was perspiring enough to water the tumbleweed fields. This was not a day for a corduroy dress. I wished I had worn a pair of shorts and a cotton blouse like Lynn. Lynn always knew what to wear. She dressed in simple clothing and was fashionable always – a simple elegance fashionable. I always felt like I dressed too convoluted and too much. That day I certainly did have on too much. Right at that moment I wanted to take off my ruffled crinolines and my shoes. Why didn't I wear sandals? The pink patent leather was hot and scalding my feet. I decided when I got back to town, I was going to take some shorts and a blouse out of the store's stock and put them on and go barefoot. It was a country store, so it didn't matter.

I walked down the opposite side of the road towards where we had parked. We had to park quite a distance away because the rest of the townspeople had gotten there before we did. The equipment trucks and transportation vehicles formed a solid wall between the road on one side and the cornfield beyond. The filming couldn't be seen from the road, so when I looked back as I was walking, I couldn't tell if they were taking a break yet, or not. I was

RJ Buckley

getting nervous. It was late. We should have started back already.

I reached for the door handle and discovered the car was locked.

"Oh no!" I exclaimed out loud as I put both hands on top of my head and spun in a circle. There was no shade. I looked back down the road towards the trucks and saw nothing that appeared to be anyone taking any breaks. All the people were still on the other side of the barricade of tall vehicles. And no one was leaving for their cars.

I began pacing. I couldn't take my shoes off because of the hot ground and the spiky stickers that usually hid under the dirt's surface. There were big red ants all over the place, too - the stinging type. I walked over to the ditch that was on the other side of the car. There was a trickle of water in its bottom and some grass had grown up near the edge. So, I took off my shoes and wiped my feet on the grass, cooling them. There wasn't a tree in sight. Nothing.

102

"Come on, Lynn! Come on!" I said outload as I spun in a circle again, displaying frustration and impatience. My first thought was to go back and get her. But then I knew how much she had wanted to talk to George, so I resigned myself to the fact that I was just going to be late and that I'd have to face the consequences. I was almost 18 and I didn't feel that my father should be so unreasonable, anyway. I was getting married, for god's sake!

I put on my shoes and went to the car and leaned against it, facing the street. My hair had gone limp with the heat and sweat, so I took off the head band, slipped it up on my arm, and leaned over and shook my hair while running my fingers through it. Next, I fluffed my skirt, trying to get some air to circulate underneath. If I would have had a place to put the crinolines, I'd take them off.

Quite a distance up the road to my left, maybe 15 car lengths or more, a man stepped out of a black limo. The opening door caught my attention and I watched him stand there looking in my direction. He was easy to see because there weren't any other cars or people that far down on my side of the road away from the equipment trucks and trailers. He began walking towards me. He was wearing gray dress slacks and a white dress shirt, opened at the neck, sleeves rolled up a couple turns. I could see he was tan and tall. Good physique. He continued walking towards me.

Omigosh! It is Cary Grant! No, it can't be. He's not here. It must be his double. But then where is Lynn? Where is she? I began to panic.

"Hello," he said to me from about four yards away.

"Hi." *It's him, it's really him!*

"Do you live near here?" He came within three feet of me and stopped.

"Uh . . . yep, I do. In Wasco, east of here. About 25 miles."

104

"That's a lovely pink dress. It is corduroy, isn't it?"

"Yep. Corduroy. Not really a summer dress. But it matches my shoes."

"Yes, I can see that. Lovely shoes. Patent leather. I have patent leather shoes."

"Pink ones?" *That's a dumb thing to say!* "I mean . . . I . . . well, I didn't mean that you would wear pink."

"I do wear pink. But not pink shoes," he laughed and cocked his head. "How old are you?"

"Eighteen. Almost eighteen."

He reached for my left hand, "Do I see an engagement ring on your finger?"

"Uh . . . yep. I am getting married in December." *You stupid ninny, why didn't you say you inherited it from a dead Aunt?*

"Getting married so young. Are you truly in love?" He was still holding my hand and smiling down at me, his gray-blue eyes looking into mine.

I wanted to say no, that I was in love with him and that I'd run away with him right that instant, if he wanted. All he had to do was ask. But instead, I said, "I guess I am. I don't know for sure."

"Well, you should be sure before you marry. You're a very charming young lady. What is your name?"

"Rebecca McMullen." He was still holding my hand and I was feeling uneasy, not knowing what to do. I tried relaxing my hand, but that felt awkward.

He must have sensed my dilemma because he patted my hand held in his and then let go.

"Are you waiting for someone?"

"Yep, my girlfriend. She knows your double."

"Oh, really? How does she know him?"

"The riding academy in San Fernando. She goes there, too."

"Ah! Well, he is quite the horseman and stunt man. Have you had lunch?"

"Nope. I skipped lunch so we could come here, now I have to get back to the store and go to work. I am so afraid my dad is on his way here. He said he'd come after me if I was gone longer than two hours, and now it's been two and a half. I wish she would hurry up. I'm going to be in trouble." *Shut up, quit rambling!*

I noticed his hesitation and curious grin, while he seemed to scan my face and then held his gaze for a moment, looking directly into my eyes again, almost as if he was about to ask a question. I felt vibrations and a presence I'd never felt before. Out of the corner of my eye I saw movement.

It was Lynn, running across the road towards us. Then I saw other people returning to their cars.

"It appears you'll be leaving now," he reached for my hand again, lifted it and kissed it. "I hope you'll be happy. I love your pink corduroy dress." He turned and walked back to his car.

I was stunned and paralyzed. I didn't feel the sun's heat anymore, I didn't feel sorry about being late, I didn't care, and I was never going to wash my hand again.

"That was Cary Grant!" Lynn cried out as she got closer.

"Yep, it was. He likes my pink corduroy dress."

"He said that?"

"Yep . . . and you know what?"

"What?"

"The wedding's off!" Well, I didn't say that, but I wanted to.

Jim and I were married that December in 1958 at the First Baptist Church in Wasco. We had a lovely church wedding, the choir sang, my long-time piano teacher played the organ. It was beautiful. My wedding dress was a gift from my Aunt Mabel, and she also had her French seamstress make my sister Mary's wedding dress a couple years later too. Mine was French lace over satin, fitted floor-length, a 'fish-tail' flounce, with lace arm coverings, and a beautiful veil. I felt like a princess.

After the wedding we'd planned to drive to Las Vegas for our honeymoon. I find it amusing that Vegas has played an integral part of my life over the years, through my marriages, since age 18 till now at the age of 81.

So, we left after the reception in Jim's hopped-up, ice blue, pick-up truck with white walls, and chrome stacks on each side of the cab, Vegas-bound. But Jim was tired, so we decided to stay in Mojave, a desert crossroads settlement at that time. I was so nervous about our first night together, had no idea what, when, and how to consummate the marriage.

Then came the memorable moment … it was the first time I ever saw a man's penis. On my wedding night! Can you believe it? Here we were - the bride and groom, Ding and Dong! But when I saw his dong, I didn't have a clue about what I was supposed to do. Or he was supposed to do. We'd done nothing together but had a few kisses during the months before we married, no petting, no nothing. And to see this … this thing sticking straight out at me when I came out of the bathroom swishing my new white chiffon bridal shower peignoir set, like it's done in the movies, I didn't know whether to backup and lock myself in the bathroom, or run, or yell for my mother, or for a doctor. I thought Jim had a deformity attached to his groin, and it looked like it was about to burst. Lordy!

I don't believe I've ever fully recovered from the shock of seeing that first penis. I know my poor husband never recovered from my reaction, at least in our marriage.

"What do we do now?" we both asked in unison, staring at each other.

We knew we had to figure it out, but we were literally puzzled. It was okay, whatever IT was, because now we were married, whatever THAT was. I equated marriage with my girl and boy paper doll fantasies - living together in a paper house and having perfect meals in the dining room with perfect flowers in the middle of the table. A dollhouse world. I had visualized having guests over for a party or watching television in the family room, the wife waving at the husband as he left for work every morning in the family car. I saw nothing beyond that. I didn't have a damn clue about marriage or sex. And you aren't going to believe this, neither did Jim.

I didn't even know how to cook. So, here we have an 18-year-old girl, who just retired her paper dolls, and an 18-year-old boy who sat on the edge of the bed in a motel room with a stiff prick not knowing what to do with it, desperately looking at my horrified face.

Well, we tried this, and we tried that, all in a pitch dark room, of course. Fumbling, bumbling, wondering, and finally quitting, mostly in embarrassment. We just couldn't get the damn thing to do anything or go wherever it was supposed to go. I wasn't sure what it was supposed to do to me, or where, for I'd never looked at myself down there, my mother told me not to. And I certainly wasn't going to do it now and wasn't going to let him touch or look.

So, we gave up and went to sleep. Next day when we got to Vegas, we went to a bookstore. Great city to be when neither one of us drank or gambled or fucked. And we only had 150 silver dollars from a silver dollar tree given to us at our wedding reception.

But we were determined to figure out this sex thing, because his guy pals had been teasing him about it, and my gal pals had been all giggly and twittery, as if they knew anything. By God! We were going to do it one way or another!

Who would ever think it would cause so much frustration? I was perfectly content before this friggin' thing came into my life and totally changed it.

Okay, so we went to the bookstore looking for pictures or diagrams to show us what the hell to do. Yea, right! Every book we found that even came close would lead you right up to the point of penetration, but didn't tell you what to do, exactly where to put it. Where the hell was it supposed to go? Surely, we weren't the stupidest people on the earth? It went nowhere on me! Where was a copy of the Complete Illustrated Kama Sutra, when it was needed? (My eighth husband had two copies, one in each nightstand by his bed. I wonder if he knew what to do when he was eighteen.)

For Jim the First and I, it was like, "Drive the fuckin' 18-wheeler into a compact car space!" or "Put a 5-pound tube of salami in a hot dog bun!" It was too big to go anywhere on me. (But of course, it was average size. I was the problem.)

Do you have any idea how humiliating that must have been to my husband too? I was sorry about that. But, he was supposed to know those things. His friends had done it before, why didn't they tell him? Why didn't he ask? Why didn't he know? Wasn't that the man's responsibility?

Well, we gave up at the bookstore, went back to the motel room and I called my mother. She laughed so effing hard, I told her to give the phone to daddy, it wasn't funny. She handed off the phone. Amazing! I then proceeded to ask my father how to fuck. OMG! And it was even more mind-blowing that he took the time to explain it to me. In detail, dammit! Now I was mortified to unprecedented heights!

I wanted out of this marriage. Didn't want to have anything to do with it. This just wasn't going to work. It was too much, and too damn distressing! And Daddy's step by step fuck plan didn't work anyway. So, we packed up, cut the honeymoon short - that's laughable, and went back home to Jim's parents' house.

Long story short, I ended up in a Bakersfield hospital for a procedure after Jim left for his advanced training in Georgia. Without sex.

I was totally stressed out. The hymen had to be cut and dilated under an anesthesia. The doctor said I was the first patient he'd ever seen who had to be knocked out for the treatment. Of course, he didn't know I could never wear a Tampon either, because the one and only time I tried to insert one, I fainted dead off the toilet onto the floor. Sticking things into my vagina just wasn't my forte. I was into topical masturbation, but nothing more than that.

I don't know why my parents worried so much about me when I was in high school, but I am sure everyone thought I had screwed with all the boys I dated. Sure, I was a big flirt, I will admit that, but you can imagine how they were surprised at my little surgery problem. The news spread like wildfire. Need I say I was glad of that? Ha!

And my husband must have been disconcerted to no end, because I sure as hell didn't see that "thing" of his much after that. He must have felt like he was at fault, despite my under-developed twat.

Moving on … we finally actually did the deed six months after we were married. But then I couldn't understand why and what all the fuss and anticipation was about. I felt like it was a bother and didn't like it. Mother was right! Was it the power of suggestion, maybe?

He preferred masturbation and as a matter of fact, so did I. On our own selves, on our own time. Although he asked me to do him on occasion. I didn't like that either, one wrist would get tired, and I'd have to change hands. It took him so long, and was so boring. Not normal, our sex-life was not even close. But I had no idea what it was supposed to be. No comparisons.

We had friend-fun, of course. We were pals. We moved to his first Army assignment at White Sands Missile Range in New Mexico, he didn't make it through paratrooper training, they discovered he was color-blind and assigned him to be a Colonel's driver at White Sands.

We lived in Las Cruces. I loved it. My first travel adventure. On weekends we explored the southern areas of New Mexico, day trips. Saw the sights. We laughed, showed excitement at discovering something new. It was adventurous and fulfilling for me.

We even did food runs at night to the orchards and fields around Las Cruces in Billy the Kid country, to collect vegetables and fruits from the ground and trees to last till payday when we could buy groceries at the supermarket. We didn't know how to budget the $160 monthly allotment from the Army. His direct pay of $90+ went towards the apartment rent and part of the truck payment. So, everything else had to come out of the 160: utilities, auto insurance, gasoline, food, entertainment, etc. We didn't do so well; the money would be gone two weeks into the month. That left fried potatoes, spaghetti, and peanut butter sandwiches the last two weeks AND whatever we could find foraging the fields.

The time came when we realized I needed to find a job to supplement our income. And since Las Cruces was a university town as well as military, jobs were scarce.

I applied at the Mountain States Telephone Company for a Long-Distance Operator position. There weren't any openings, but they said they'd keep me on file. In the meantime, I took a job with a private nursing home, as an aide - 39 cents an hour, 9 hours a day, 30 minutes for lunch, two 10-minute breaks. My first job, since working for my dad at the five and dime in Wasco, was to clean bathrooms, mop floors, bathe terminal patients, change their diapers, and change the beds in my assigned rooms. I never complained and was happy to befriend and have conversations with the elderly patients that were still conscious. They were all terminal and bedridden, at their final stop in life. So sad. After nine months working there, the phone company called and offered me a job. More money and sitting all day or night in a chair taking long distance calls.

So, then our life became more normal, a routine of Jim being away during the day, me working the night shifts – being a newbie. Still no sex to speak about.

But I worked with a bunch of women who talked about men, husbands, boyfriends, and sex continually. I hadn't experienced anything they were talking about, and didn't join the conversations, but listened to every damn word.

There came a time when the discussion of having a baby came up. That seemed to be the next plateau of marriage, even though we hadn't even mastered and completed the first one. But we were still friends, buddies, and had set up house. We then had intercourse occasionally to make a baby, despite how difficult that was. We did it for the specific purpose to make a baby. Not for pleasure, but to impregnate me under the covers in the dark of night – the only way we knew how.

As I am writing, my sexual escapades over the years after that come to mind, only to remind

me of how ignorant I was in that first marriage.
Totally in the dark. I mean literal dark. Oh, I knew
about self-manipulation and the good feelings it
led to but didn't know how it could be a benefit to
me in *intercourse* (hate that word). Jim was finally
able to gain benefit without masturbation, but not
I. It was a while before the possibilities in store for
me inevitably came. But back then, it was way too
early for the sex education gleaned from the
onslaught of husbands and other lovers resulted.
Jim missed out on all that.

We had a quiet, calm life in Las Cruces,
New Mexico. Most of our spare time together was
spent continuing to live out our teens, going on
drives to historical places and sight-seeing in most
of New Mexico, as well as over the borders into
Mexico and Texas on day trips. And occasionally
making the 17-hour drive back to California on a
long weekend when we could get the time off

together. Otherwise, it was work, eat, sleep during the week, day trips when we had time off together. It became an acceptable lifestyle, was rather easy. We didn't ask for much, didn't expect much. I wrote lengthy letters, sometimes 20 tablet pages, to parents, sisters, grandmothers, aunts and cousins, I think maybe to a couple high school gal pals too. Writing letters was my way to communicate my thoughts before computers and before life became so complex, convoluted, and complicated. I wasn't thinking of the future in those days, other than wondering at times what we were going to do when Jim's three years in the Army were over. But I did wonder why I wasn't getting pregnant. Several of my co-workers at the telephone company were sporting baby bumps. Talk was of nothing else at work. But the months rolled by without me missing one of my dreadful periods.

Dreadful … meaning I'd spend the first two or three days of the eight-day cycle every month in bed vomiting with a migraine-like headache and horrific low abdominal cramps. I'd ply myself with over-the-counter pain pills, to no avail. Sleep and heating-pad were the best remedies. Even back in school I was absent at least two days a month, and at work the same, until I was almost 21 and delivered my first child. Then the sickness and pain all stopped. Who knew?

So, finally we took our question to a military doctor on base. Why weren't we pregnant? He did an exam and came up with a solution. I was to take one-a-day pills to stop my monthly period for nine months. It was a new pharma still in trials. His premise was that my system would build itself up since I had such hard *ministrations* (hate that word too), with the goal of becoming pregnant when I stopped taking the pills. He also explained we would have to have sexual intercourse as often as we could after that. Especially at ovulation time. I learned more at that doctor's visit than I had in all the time leading up to it. I was thrilled I didn't have to have any over-flowing two-Jumbo-Kotex-pad days for nine months, and no vomiting headaches or cramps. Later I learned that the medication was the forerunner of the birth control pill.

So that's what I did, and I became pregnant ten months later. Success! Nine months later James Barry was born with induced labor, took a very short time, I think under five hours. Both sets of grandparents came from California to see their first grandson. Barry was born in June 1961, Jim's time in the Army was over in September.

Our three years in New Mexico were pleasant enough, we were still so young - young minds and tastes, young opinions, young actions. Jim turned 21 four months before me, a couple weeks after Barry was born (both Gemini). We returned to California by my 21st birthday to live in a little one-bedroom duplex up in the hills of Camarillo. Still adjusting to parenting, and now leading a civilian life, both having to find jobs, and a baby-sitter. But we were very lucky … Jim was hired by his cousin in a Chevron service station; I was hired by my mother-in-law Hazel's boss to work as a cashier in the grocery store with her. And Jim's aunt Kathryn babysat Barry. So, there we were. Starting a new life together, but still feeling like teenagers.

Jim worked double shifts and fell right back into being buddies with his high school cohorts, harmless guy stuff. I worked and was a mother after my shifts. We hardly had any time alone together, other than sleep. The days were the same one after the other. We would play cards with his relatives on their weekly poker nights and join his parents to eat Mexican food at their favorite Mexican restaurant in Oxnard on Tuesday nights. They bowled on Friday nights in Thousand Oaks, and one season I joined the team with them. I enjoyed the regular family activities, but I don't recall any independent activities during that time, away from family. And still our sex-life was pretty much nonexistent. He was always tired, and I didn't mind at all.

We lived like a brother and sister. Pals, visiting his parents and family (who, thank goodness, I adored). We went to work every day, but didn't share our feelings about anything to each other. Hardly any conversation about work or anything else was initiated by either of us. Maybe there wasn't anything to talk about.

Of course, I didn't want to share conversation with him about my flirting and crush on my Chinese boss's nephew, who worked part-time at one of the two Chinese markets they owned locally, who came from China to attend UCLA. Or my flirting with Jim's cousin's partner at the gas station when I'd stop for a fill-up. Yep, I can only speak for myself, for I've no idea how Jim was feeling.

I only know something was missing, couldn't put a finger on it at the time, but felt I was dangling out there on my own. Didn't know what to do. Felt like there should be more to being married than there was. I didn't feel any thrills like I did in high school kissing my boyfriends or being hugged by them. Or the attention they gave me, the looks on their faces. That was absent from our relationship.

It wasn't obvious at the time, but it was attraction that was missing, mine to him. I am surmising here. No adoring love and attraction between the two of us. Again, I am speaking for myself. Sad, but true. Felt friendship, though.

By the way, while living in Camarillo before we split up, we went to Hollywood a couple times, which was only an hour away. We drove there to have dinner and afterwards go to a movie in one of several beautiful theatres of the period. One night we decided to go to see a double feature: Deep Throat, a Linda Lovelace film, and The Devil and Mrs. Jones. They were showing at a famous adult theater in Hollywood. We both were curious; thought we might learn something; everybody was talking about Deep Throat. But it didn't open up any avenues to do our marriage any good. In fact, I thought the movie was funny, and we both were embarrassed and started feeling uncomfortable in the theater. We left halfway through; it was enough.

The short of it, the end of our marriage began happening when I became attracted to and curious about others and didn't want to be with Jim anymore. I didn't act on my curiosity, didn't cheat on him, just continued flirting until I felt I must leave before something would happen. I wasn't thinking about the sex, though, just thought about the thrilling feeling again of embraces, kisses, having fun as I did before in high school. It was incredible that I was so naïve and immature, even at age 21 with a baby in tow. I felt I needed to get away from my boss's nephew and from Jim's boss too, those infatuations were growing.

So, one day I telephoned my parents and asked them to come after me and Barry (he was a year old), that I didn't want to be married anymore. They said they would come the next day and would rent a trailer to haul whatever I needed. I was ready when they got there, didn't take any kitchen stuff or furnishings, only took baby stuff and my personal belongings.

I left a note for Jim saying I wasn't happy and had gone to live with mother and daddy in Morro Bay. They had opened a new store there, while we were in New Mexico. In the note I suggested he give whatever furnishings he didn't want or need to his mother. Said I was sorry, but I didn't want to be married anymore.

And that was that!

Startling moment of truth was when Jim's boss called a few weeks later, saying he was coming north to a military reservist summer camp and would like to take me to dinner. Of course, he was married, and it frightened me to no end, because I was so attracted to his Bogart looks and the way he flirted with me. I said no thank you and told my father if he called again, to tell him anything, but I didn't want to ever talk to the man again.

But it wasn't over with Jim yet …

CHAPTER 8

Other Lovers

Bert B.

Ron P.

Errol R.

My continuous random thoughts about anything and everything drive me nuts, all the time. From the moment I wake up in the morning to the last thought before dropping off to sleep late nights or the wee hours of the next day. Thoughts of family and friends – dead and alive, thoughts of sickness that affects us all, thoughts of future

131

goals, thoughts of to-do lists for the day/week/month, thoughts of food, housekeeping, hobbies (travel, music, painting, collecting, decorating), marketing my books, updating websites and blogs, AND OF COURSE WRITING!

My over-crowded mind is playing its broken record over and over. You would think it would tire of the repetition by now. However, I will say, I thank my lucky stars that Dementia and Alzheimer's hasn't set in. To me that's when the mind says, "That's it, I am through!" In that respect, I am grateful my mind isn't through. So, on with the memories …

BERT B.

As soon as Bert found out I had left my first husband and was living with my parents in Morro Bay, he telephoned. Asked if he could come over to see me the following weekend, take me out to dinner. I said of course and was excited to see him. I had thought of him quite a lot and felt bad about what happened on my porch the night I broke off the engagement. Now I was without the fear of intimacy, now I was an "experienced woman", not the schoolgirl I once was. But I was still super-duper naive.

So, he came early and took me to lunch at the Golden Tee Restaurant at the golf course. We talked and talked, catching up on our lives since high school. Then we rode around for a while, parked and resumed our high school kissing and petting activity, which thrilled me more than it did before. Then as it began to get dark, he took me to an isolated spot in Morro dunes and spread a blanket. Yep, you're right. We made love half on the blanket and half in the sand. I'd never felt that way with Jim, I loved Bert's body connected to mine, him holding me. But when he had an orgasm, of course I didn't. And I didn't care because I could always have my own later, alone. I felt like I'd fallen in love all over again with him. I was starry-eyed and wondered when I was going to see him again. He took me home; we said our goodbyes and he left for Bakersfield. I wondered for a moment about the dinner that he'd mentioned before he came, but figured the lunch was the replacement.

Anyway, I wrote him every day, told him I loved him, told him I bought an early Christmas present for him, would save it till then. He was on my mind all the time. A month later he called my sister Mary, who lived in Shafter near Bakersfield, and asked her to tell me he was getting married, he couldn't tell me himself.

Well, that telephone call from Mary devastated me. I cried and cried. But weeks later I realized he must have hurt just as much when I rejected him. Back in '58 when it happened, my father had told me the next day Bert came to the store with tears in his eyes wanting to know what he had done and what he could do to get me back. So now four years later it crossed my mind that Bert might be getting even, or maybe he had to go through with the wedding plans not expecting me to leave my husband, or maybe he didn't like making love with me – I was very insecure about my inexperience, or … all the possible other reasons that flooded my mind. He never explained.

After a week of crying at the least bit of provocation, I decided I deserved the shun, and I put it out of my mind and went on, essentially turning off my feelings. I became quite adept at that in the years to follow. That year I gave Bert's Christmas present to my dad. Bert married and had two daughters. But our time was not over.

RON P.

I first met Ron P. when I began working for Safeway Stores as a checker. I applied there after Bert's one day stand. But had been working in daddy's five and dime; he had opened one in Morro Bay after leaving Wasco. Safeway finally hired me since I had grocery checker experience in Camarillo at the two Chinese markets, and I had years of experience cashiering for my father in Sprouse Reitz Stores in Wasco and then in Morro Bay - next door to Safeway. So, Safeway sent me to their checker school in Los Angeles for a week and I returned as a full-fledged certified grocery checker. Ron P. was a box-boy, just out of high school.

I was almost 23, Ron was 18. Chronological age didn't matter in our case, for he was much more mature than I was. He'd graduated from high school and was biding his time working as a box-boy, trying to figure out what he wanted to do with the rest of his life. His mother was a barber, owned her own shop, and wanted Ronnie to join her in the business, even offered to put him through Barber College. But Ronnie wasn't ready to make that decision. He was having the time of his life, partying and playing with the girls. That was his priority, parties and girls.

My life's path up to that point had been quite different than his. I'd been married and had a son and had a hurtful rejection the prior year.

But Ron kept me smiling and laughing all the time in our checker-to-box-boy relationship. I found myself eager to go to work just because he was there. I was sad when he wasn't, when he had a day off. His teasing and suggestive behavior had become addictive. He'd lower his long dark eyelashes and give me a sexy look that would thrill to the core. I wasn't the only one who was affected by his playfulness. I watched the young girls file into the store to flirt with him. And he certainly gave them what they wanted.

One day he asked me for a date.

"I can't go out with you, you're too young," I told him.

"How old are you?"

"I am 22."

"So. I am almost 19. That makes you only three years older than me. That's not much. Besides, I'm more experienced than you, so that makes me older."

"Oh? Is that so? What makes you think you're more experienced?" I was laughing by this time.

"I can tell."

"I do not think so."

All the time we were talking I was ringing up the groceries on the cash register and he was boxing them. The customers were talking to each other, so they weren't paying attention to the two of us bantering back and forth.

"So, how many men have you made love to?"

I couldn't believe he had asked me that.

"So? How many?"

I darted a look of disdain at him, "Are you crazy?" But I relaxed when I saw the mischievousness in his eyes and laughed again. "That's none of your business."

"I bet I've made love more than you have."

"That wouldn't surprise me a bit. Now, let's change this subject, please."

And that was the way it went. He'd come out with some of the darndest questions and statements I'd ever heard in my very young naive life. He was right on the button, though.

I'd only been sexual with two men by then, my husband of three years, and Bert once. And during the marriage, if Jim and I made love once every two to three months, that was exorbitant.

I wasn't really all that thrilled with the act, though; it didn't do anything for me. My husband

139

and I were the same age, and we were more like pals than husband and wife. I sometimes think we never should have married. But then, my dear beloved son Barry wouldn't have been a part of my life. Remember, I was 18 and just out of high school when we married, so was he, and I certainly wasn't ready to be a wife and mother. For me, it was too young. As I walked down the aisle, I knew it was wrong.

Now here I was, in my twenties, kidding around with an 18-year-old that was sexual in his intent and demeanor. Not overtly, but quietly suggestive. Insinuation mostly. Totally opposite to Jim.

And when Ron and I were on duty together, he always boxed my customers' groceries first. (In the early '60s groceries were boxed instead of bagged.) We had quite a flirting exchange going on, of course, and I'd met more than my match in

Ron. Happier than I'd been in a while. I liked the tease and flirting. Life felt exciting again.

When I look back over my life today, I realize it was mostly about the excitement and new experiences. It's that way even now. Not the excitement being with the opposite sex, now it's the excitement of my surroundings and writing and travel. But still crave excitement! I envision I will 'till my dying moment.

In 1963, being around Ron lifted my spirits, and I looked forward to seeing him every day.

Our flirting was mostly kidding and surface talk, however, certainly wasn't thinking of dating or having a relationship with anybody, being newly separated. Especially with a box boy. I laugh. Younger than me. Right out of high school. Hell no! We were just a checker and box boy team having fun kibitzing and flirting while we worked.

But over time it began developing into something more. He constantly said to me, 'age does not matter, it is okay.' He seemed older than me, as a matter of fact, and I began to believe he was.

One day Ron told me he had decided to go to barber school, was going to work in his mother's barber shop – Rose's. His mother would come shopping in the store, and of course, she would come through my check stand. I was impressed at how cheerful she was, and liked her from the get-go. His younger sister Bernadette, with the tiny voice, was so cute. I liked her immediately too. That was the extent of his family in Morro Bay. His mother was Hispanic, divorced from a Czechoslovakian husband who lived in the San Joaquin Valley. Ron's aunt Virginia, Rose's sister, had married an Armenian rancher in the Fresno area. So, Ron had cousins too, all inland, three hours from Morro Bay.

One weekend, my girlfriend Mary Lee, and I went to a Saturday night community dance at the

142

Vet's Hall in the neighboring town of Cayucos, a couple miles up the coast. Mary Lee was a hairdresser and worked in a salon next to my folks' five and dime in the Safeway shopping center. We had met when I went there to have my hair cut on a lunch hour. Mary Lee worked in the salon, Ron and I worked at Safeway, my folks in Sprouse Reitz. It was one big happy family, all of us working in that square of stores and shops.

On that Saturday night when we entered the Vet's Hall, Ronnie was slow dancing with a young girl who hadn't graduated from high school, yet. She appeared to be all of 15 or 16 years old. But then, he was only 18, so it was appropriate.

Mary Lee saw him first. "Look who's here, Becky. By the bandstand." She raised her eyebrows and grinned, "If he gets any closer, he'll be on the other side of her." We both laughed.

I watched him slow dance through that one, the next one, and the next. He was a sexy dancer, as

143

well as rhythmic. Not a whole lot of movement, though, just slow and easy, even on the fast songs.

"We should go ask him to dance," Mary Lee said. "Shake him up a bit. Want to?" She was my age and would always tease Ronnie when she came into the market. She had a quick, funny answer to anything he had to say. It was a riot listening to them go at each other.

"Oh, I don't know. I don't think so. If you want to dance with him, go ahead. I will just sit here and have my drink. Go ahead. Really."

I began sipping my 7-Up. Alcoholic beverages weren't served at those summer dances because it was open to teenagers. But that didn't stop some of them from going out to their cars and having beer or wine. Hard liquor didn't seem to be popular with the young people that I knew in those days. Beer was the drink of the day, mostly. I didn't like beer, but I'd sip it at parties, sometimes. And I'd have a wine cooler occasionally in bars with Mary Lee. But never hard liquor.

Next thing I knew, Ronnie was standing in front of me.

"Let's dance," he said as he reached for me.

"I don't know how. I never learned," And that was the truth. I shrank back from his reach.

"I can teach you." He was grinning from ear to ear, took the drink from my hand, set it on the empty chair next to me, and pulled me to my feet.

I began laughing nervously, resisting the pull.

He placed one of my hands on his shoulder, then he grabbed the other and held it in the proverbial dance pose. With his free hand in the small of my back, he pulled me close to his body. We just stood there; pressed together.

"How does that feel?" he asked with twinkling eyes.

"It feels like you're trying to suffocate me."

"Well, I am."

"This isn't going to work," I said. "I'll step all over your toes."

"I don't care."

"So, what do we do now?" I asked.

"We wait until the music starts."

After that dance, I wanted to leave, it was too stressful for me. Because I never learned properly how to dance, I felt like such a klutz. Mary Lee and I went elsewhere to the over-21 crowds and watched people.

After that, one day at work, Ron asked to take me out to dinner and another dance at the Cayucos Vets Hall. Our first date.

We had dinner next door to the Hall, a small café that specialized in fish. It was pleasant and he was easy to talk to. I saw more of another side of Ron, a normal guy, not flirty and sexual. We laughed a lot at dinner, he with his beautiful slanted eyes. I grinned just being with him, it was comfortable. After dinner we went over to the dance hall by the pier.

Cayucos is a quaint beach town on the Central Coast of California, between Morro Bay and Cambria. It has a small bay, a pier, and sandy beaches, beach shops, bars, and restaurants. In those days it was the summer go-to beach for the central valley residents to make the two-hour-drive escape from three-digit heat.

I don't remember if it was a live band or not, that night, it probably was. But I was uncomfortable there with the teenagers. Ron asked me to dance, and I did try again.

I never went to dances in high school, wasn't allowed to, so didn't learn. My parents were opposed to it; I think it had to do with our church at the time. Anytime there was a dance at school for any reason, my folks came and picked me up before it. I couldn't even go in to watch.

Such silliness! And first husband Jim didn't dance either.

So, here I was with a guy who was half Latin and full of musical talent and rhythm, and I couldn't even dance a step. I must have been a bore. I didn't know it at the time, but he also played the guitar. Well, I played the piano and sang, for myself. And in high school I sang in the glee club, and played tenor sax in the marching band, so I wasn't a total loss. Ha ha. I just couldn't dance.

But Ron had me under his spell and taught me to slow dance, which I've done forever after. The only dance I know. He danced slow and close. Bodies touching from chests to thighs, tightly. We were nearly the same height. I'd never experienced dancing that close before Ron. And very rarely since.

Well, inevitably, his car became a bed for us after our dates of slow dancing. He lived with his mom, and I lived with my parents. I understand my parents fear of me going to dances, now. But still it depends on the kids, many kids danced in high school and didn't end up having sex afterwards. Right? I don't know if they did or not. Ha! Didn't ask.

Then one night we went to a house party out on Atascadero Road, in the hills between Morro Bay and Atascadero. A private party with alcohol. Ron took a six-pack of short cans of Country Club beer. I didn't like to drink, especially beer, it smelled bad to me. But we had so much fun with his friends, I asked for one of the beers. And then another one which did me in. I was truly a lightweight. Two short cans? He helped me to the car, and we commenced to make 'mad passionate' love. Man, oh man, did we ever! Of course, I was all for making him happy, and moved in ways he couldn't help but have an organism. I wasn't on the pill; he didn't wear a prophylactic.

Yes, indeed-y! It happened! That night. In the car. The teenager and the cougar. I didn't have a period after that. I was pregnant.

But I ignored all the signs, pretended to myself it would go away. It had to be something else.

Ron and I dated a few more times, but then it waned. I was running from him and running from the pregnancy.

ERROL R.

Then came another lovely guy into my life. A gentle sort, happy-go-lucky, very attentive man, named Errol R. We were both born in 1940. He worked in construction, and I met him while I was employed by the Morro Bay branch of Bank of America. I quit working for Safeway. Errol and I began dating, but he also had a son with another gal that he was involved with. That's happened a couple times with single men I've dated, they had babies with someone else and didn't marry, but helped support them, good guys.

Errol grinned a lot and his perfect white teeth set off his sexy blue eyes with long lashes. What was it with these guys with long, sexy eye lashes? They had them naturally, with no assistance! And he had thick, brown hair. He wasn't tall, was stout, and dressed in western attire. Blue jeans and snap western style, long-sleeved shirts. Most of the guys in construction, I noticed at the time, dressed that way. He would come to my teller window if his prior girlfriend was busy. She worked there too. I learned a lot about him from her, she never spoke ill of him.

Errol was an only son of a very successful real estate broker. His mother imbibed too much, but they were of the social strata that drank and partied, socialized for business and pleasure. They both loved their son. I enjoyed being around them,

151

went places with them. One trip was to a new horseracing track in L.A. that they had invested in, owned a stake. They also owned part of the aforementioned restaurant/bar/motel/music venue called the Golden Tee in Morro Bay. I loved going there.

I must admit Errol was the most pleasant of all the men I dated at that time. We laughed, drank, dined, and sexed. No complaints. But of course, I was still ignoring the fact I was pregnant.

RETURN TO RON P.

The pretense and dating others went on for a couple more months. And I continued to work until I began thickening through the middle – five months pregnant. I finally told Ron that I was pregnant. He immediately said we would get married. In a way I was excited about that, although I knew it would be a problem with my mother and father. They didn't know that I'd dated Ron. His mother and sister knew, and our friends knew, but my family and their friends didn't.

I didn't mention the prejudices of my folks with blacks and browns. Could have been with yellows and reds, too. Any race different than ours. (But I am happy to say they dropped those prejudices over the years.) But I didn't mention it to Ron.

One weekend soon after that, Barry and I rode along to the San Joaquin Valley to visit Ron's aunt Virginia and his cousins. His mother Rose took us in her roomy Lincoln Continental – loved that car. And I'd such a wonderful time with the whole family at the ranch and at a lake nearby. We decided that because I was still married to Jim, hadn't filed divorce yet, that we could go to Mexico and get the divorce, then we would get married. I didn't know how that worked, but I went along with what everyone was suggesting.

Rose and Virginia took us to Mexico and found an attorney that did quickie divorces. Rose paid for it. But I started worrying about having to tell mother and daddy, not only that I was pregnant, but I was going to marry Ron. I felt there was a little more time left to figure it out.

All the time the baby was growing inside of me I refused to acknowledge it. I don't know what I was thinking, how could I ignore the fact that I was pregnant? I've no idea. I hadn't been to a doctor yet. Did I think that it would just disappear? Another month passed. There were moments when I panicked. Late evenings especially. I'd be filled with anxiety and panic … *what should I do … how can I tell my parents?*

My son and I were living in an upstairs apartment over a garage at that time. It was a one bedroom furnished apartment, cute place. Ron would come over to visit after I told him I was going to have a baby, so my parents never saw him.

All the way back from Mexico, I was thinking of how I could handle my relationship with Ron, and how I'd tell my parents that we were going to get married because I was pregnant. A real dilemma.

I was afraid of the one remaining hurdle, Ron being half Mexican. He resembled his mother with brown skin and black hair and dark eyes. I was afraid of my parents' reaction. They knew him from Safeway, but not his association with me ... more than an association.

I remember one day I was walking home from junior high school with one of my best friends, Dorothy G. The two of us had stayed after school to rehearse with the vocal quintet. Dorothy would walk as far as the store with me, and then walk south of town to the African American section where she lived.

My mother saw us coming down the alley behind the store. She ran out and screamed at me, "Becky, get in here!"

I ran to mother inside the backroom of the dime store, confused at what I'd done wrong. "What's the matter, mother?"

"You know better than to walk with that girl. You just better be glad your daddy didn't see you. Walking with a colored person! Don't you ever do that again!"

I cried for almost an hour. Dorothy was my best friend and now I couldn't be with her anymore. She was one of my best buddies.

It is moronic how parents impose their ridiculous opinions and prejudices upon their children.

I don't remember exactly how I told them about Ron. You would think I'd remember, but I don't.

I had a blue Corvair convertible that I'd bought when working at Safeway, bought the car on a payment plan. And I remember I was really panicking as I drove up the coast beyond Big Sur by myself and boo-hooing all the way. Those days I did that a lot. I didn't know what to do. How could I tell them? How could I've been so stupid to get pregnant! What was I thinking, why didn't I use protection? I worked myself into a frenzy driving all the way to Carmel. On the way back it was dark, I knew Barry was all right because he was with my parents. And I knew no matter what happened he would be safe with my parents or with his dad. Those were my thoughts as I drove into the night. I was thinking of driving off one of the cliffs.

Yes, I was thinking of suicide when I parked on one of those pull outs on Highway one, alongside the steep, curvy road that dropped to the black ocean on one side, and up the mountain on the other. I got outside of my car and looked down at the sea far below, the iridescent surf hitting the boulders. I thought of how it would feel to drive off the cliff. Would I pass out in flight? What if it wouldn't kill me? What if it would just cripple me? I didn't see how anyone could live through a crash down into those huge rocks though, but the doubt was creeping into my mind. I was getting frightened of my thoughts and frightened of the drop off the cliff. It was dark and scary, all the way around.

I got back into the car, took some deep breaths, and drove slowly down the mountain to my parents' house in Morro Bay, determined to tell them. Oh! Now I remember! I went to their house to pick up Barry and I told them - blurted it out tearfully. That's how it happened, and I was so emotional I immediately took Barry back to our apartment and went to bed, feeling better that I'd told them. Now I would deal with the rest. I'd survived my thoughts of suicide one more time. I could think forward now. Ron and I would marry, and we would raise the baby and Barry. I liked his family, and I felt like it would be a good environment for Barry, and Ron had ambitions of becoming a barber like his mother.

Those were my thoughts that night, as I recall. Then the next day mother and daddy came to my apartment. Ron was there, we were lying on the sofa together. They walked in without knocking. And daddy asked Ron to leave, said they wanted to talk to me alone. Ron left.

They had decided that I could not marry Ron, that they didn't want Barry at his young age to be subjected to another husband. And they wanted me to have the baby and adopt it out.

159

Daddy said he knew of a doctor in Port Hueneme that would handle it all. They also said that when I started showing more, I could move back into the house with them and when visitors would come, especially family, they would put me up in a motel in Paso Robles so no one would know.

I was choking back the tears through all the one-sided conversation and was so perplexed and tired of the stress, all I could say was OK. I was tired. And that's what I did. I broke it off with Ron, told him over the phone I had a miscarriage, and avoided him after that. Told him since he was so young, he would find someone else and that it wouldn't affect him that much. Told him I would have felt guilty about being pregnant and causing him to marry so young because of it.

When I started showing, I didn't wear PG clothing. Lucky for me what was popular then were those circular tent dresses. I figured I could hide the pregnancy for a little while longer. I quit Bank of America and started working in the five and dime again, relegating myself to the back room mostly. My section to take care of was the hardware department, which was at the back of the store, so I'd not be seen much. But soon it became obvious that I was pregnant, and I couldn't hide it anymore because when I walked, the frocks of course would cling to my stomach, and anyone would be able to see the baby bump that was more than a bump. It was never a bump, was never small, I ballooned as I did with Barry.

The time came when daddy made the decision for me to stay in a motel in Paso Robles since I was showing so much at seven months. Just in case any relatives visited Morro Bay, or someone local, especially the church people would figure it out. I still had my car, so Barry and I would stay in the motel in Paso Robles till closer to the time. The plan was, when I was eight months along, they would bring me back home with them, and I'd live in the apartment downstairs. A hideout. And that's what I did. I hid.

But when I moved back to Morro Bay in my parents' home, my grandmother had come to live with us, and she stayed downstairs with me. There were two bedrooms, a kitchenette and a bathroom. I enjoyed her company, I really did. She would sing hymns all the time, acapella. So, it was getting nearer and nearer the time when I was to have the baby, and I didn't give it a thought, or how it would all come about. Daddy said he had it all planned, not to worry.

The night my water broke, I panicked and went upstairs to wake up mother and daddy and to tell them that the water had broken. I was scared. It was a four-to-five-hour trip to Port Hueneme. Daddy got a couple of pillows and blankets and he told me to go and get in the car. Mother was crying and we hugged. She told me not to worry, daddy would get me there in time.

Let's back track a bit. During the pregnancy I drove to Oxnard to be interviewed by the couple who wanted to adopt a baby. That was part of the deal. Must I tell you how difficult that was? The doctor had arranged for the adoptive couple and me to meet at the attorney's office to sign the adoption contract, IF they were satisfied with my looks and answers to the questions they asked of me. It was humiliating and added to my guilt, it was almost too much to take. I sobbed all the way back to Morro Bay. And yes, I thought about telling everybody to take a flying leap! But didn't know what I'd do, how I'd pay the hospital, where I'd live and work. I wouldn't dream of putting the added stress on my parents. I didn't want to involve Ron, either. He had moved on already. And I didn't feel the same connection with him anymore. So, I went through with it.

"Ohhhhh . . . I can't stand it . . . it hurts . . . ohhhhh . . ."

"We're almost there," daddy said, reaching back over the seat. "Just one more street. I see the street now; up ahead. There's the hospital. I'll drive to the emergency door. Almost there. Hold on."

Daddy was beside himself and had been wondering if he was doing the right thing. He told me years later, before he died, that he knew he'd made the wrong decision while driving that night, but felt it was too late to back out.

I didn't talk about it with anybody or anyone else in the years that followed. I couldn't face what I'd done - what I'd done to Ronnie, what I'd done to myself, what I'd done to my baby. I buried it deep inside me. Stuffed it down so deep it was as if it never happened. I was in denial before and after she was born.

Daddy also told me years later that he had felt guilty about his decision for years. But his guilt didn't begin to compare with mine. I take full responsibility. And although he told me he was sorry; he wasn't nearly as sorry as I was for putting them through that. I don't blame Daddy, never did, for I know he did what he thought was best.

I also know I didn't have the maturity and good sense to say, "No, I am not going to give up my child." I would now, but I didn't know and feel it then.

Daddy jumped from the car and literally ran into the hospital emergency entrance. Suddenly there were all sorts of people at the door, helping me get out of the car. I can still hear myself moaning and sobbing in an involuntary steady stream, swaying between emotional and physical anguish. At times I felt as if I was fading in and out of consciousness. I believe the body has a mechanism that shuts out the pain we cannot bear and puts us in a state of semi-consciousness when we've reached our limits. I don't remember much about anything after that until in the labor room when the nurse told me, after I asked, that Daddy had gone home. Ironically, I felt abandoned.

I never asked him why he left me there, alone; because I knew he had his reasons, one of them being embarrassment and disappointment that his daughter was having a child out of wedlock, and he couldn't face that, even with the hospital staff. My parents were from an era that shunned unwed mothers. In fact, he'd chosen that doctor and that hospital because it was far enough away so that no one he knew would know.

Remember, during the last stages of the pregnancy, so no one would know I was pregnant, he had taken other precautions. Barry and I lived out of town in a motel for a month. It was an hour away and close enough for mother and daddy to deliver groceries to me, for I'd stopped working when it became obvious. I didn't have any money, except the $100 child support a month for Barry, and I used that for the car payment. Those last few months are a blur to me. I must have been semi-conscious even then. That shut-down mechanism worked right up to the end and beyond.

"Where is the father of the child?" the attending nurse asked me.

To this day I don't know what possessed me to say, "He was killed in the Vietnam war." I am assuming the nurse already knew that it was a case of "no husband" because of who the doctor was, and it was an adoption. They had to have known he specialized in unwed mothers. He even arranged the adoptions. So, I am wondering why she asked such a question. Surely, she realized how it might affect me, and that it was a cruel question to put to me, under the circumstances. But then, that was the sign of the times. The emphasis was on how awful it was to become pregnant outside of marriage, and even more so, to give the child away. The nurse had reflected that mindset with the question she asked whether she knew it or not, or maybe my guilt was at work again. And I also remember that she was very rough with the exams she gave me every few minutes - jamming her hand up inside me to check the position of the baby and to see how much I'd dilated. At least that's how it felt at the time. I don't remember much else.

I do remember the next morning when the adoptive parents came to me. The fact I had delivered one son before, had been encouraging to them. Now here they were, standing at my bedside, saying although they were hoping for a son, they were happy I'd given them another daughter. They said they had named her Tami. I turned away, couldn't talk. Tears were welling. My thoughts shot to the girl's name I'd chosen before Barry was born;

in case he was a girl … I would name her January Lynn. January Lynn, not Tami. Didn't they realize how hard it was for me to give up my baby? No. Here they were, standing there grinning and smiling and telling me how happy they were. I was crying inside and out, knowing I was doing the wrong thing, but was doing it anyway. Not their fault, I know. They thought I wanted the adoption. I'm sure I was smiling and pleasant at the signing of the papers a few months before, because that's how I've always been. I cover up the hurt so easily, until I can't control it anymore and it busts out all over.

They left and that was the last time I saw them … I never saw my daughter … until much later.

Later that day, the sweep boy, a Cal-Poly SLO student that worked in the store for my dad, arrived at the hospital to take me back to Morro Bay. More hurt piled on. I lay on the back seat and didn't say a word on the five-hour drive.

169

CHAPTER 9

Return to Husband Number One

JIM I.

When I went back to Port Hueneme to the doctor that delivered my baby girl, I was in the reception room waiting for my six weeks follow up appointment.

Up till then, I hadn't allowed myself to dwell or even think of what I had done - given up my child. I buried the thoughts of self-shaming remorse and had not spoken of the event with anybody. Not my mother, not my father. No one. It was as if it didn't happen.

I didn't think about my future, what I was going to do, where I'd live. I was still living in the apartment on the bottom floor of my parents' house, in the room next to my grandmother (Mama). She was a godsend. She kept me going, although I don't think she knew what had happened. She may have known, but never said anything.

I was looking through magazines at the doctor's office, a huge reception area, when a woman came in cradling a baby in her arms, I could only see the dark shock of hair on the baby sticking out of the blanket, but I recognized the mother. It was my baby's adoptive mother!

I panicked, grabbed my purse, heart beating out of my chest, thought I was going to pass out, and ran through the door to the exam rooms. A nurse stopped me and asked where I was going.

I answered, "I don't know … but hide me, please! I just saw my baby and her new mother …" At that point I began whimpering. Couldn't talk. The nurse helped me to one of the exam rooms and shut the door.

Right away the doc came in and said, "I am so sorry. I wasn't aware you were both scheduled at the same time. I will be with you in a moment." He left the room.

I collapsed.

After the appointment I felt very low, and the first thought that came to mind was to go see Jim in Camarillo. I don't why I even paid any attention to the thought, but I drove to Camarillo anyway, in hopes of seeing him working at the service station.

He was there. I pulled in to get gas, and he came over to my car. I still had the '63 blue Camaro convertible. It was a good feeling to see him, a peace came over me. We went to have coffee together, to talk. I am trying to remember how we ended up with his mom and dad for dinner. But we did. It was a wonderful dinner and visit, always loved Jim's parents. I bet she made chicken enchiladas with lots of olives … my favorite.

Jim and I talked about getting back together. And that seemed a tremendous relief, answer to a prayer. It would solve a lot of problems I was facing. And this time I promised myself I'd try harder to make it work. Jim was a nice guy, I knew that, and we had a son together. And I didn't want to live in Morro Bay. I felt the need to get away from there, and to relieve my mother and daddy of the burden and worries about Barry and me. This reunion would take care of that.

So, Jim and I planned to spend the next weekend together, to reacquaint, and Barry and I would stay at his folks. But that night, I spent with my grandmother (Mamaw), in El Rio (Oxnard) before going back to Morro Bay the following day. None of them knew I'd just had a baby six weeks earlier.

The following Friday I packed my bag and one for Barry to spend the weekend in Camarillo with Jim and his folks. I was feeling a bit nervous about what they knew about the baby adoption. As it turned out, the attorney that had set up the meeting with the adoptive parents had his secretary draw up the contract. She brought it into his office for signatures that day many months ago, and I recognized her. She was the wife of Jim's cousin's partner at the Chevron station. The Bogart look-alike, who called to have dinner with me after I left Jim. I was really worried about that. Didn't want Jim and his family to know. But she had not said anything to anyone, thankfully.

The weekend was wonderful, just like old times, a lot of laughs, good food and conversation, friendliness, and Barry loved it too! So, Jim and I went off by ourselves and discussed getting back together. He was working for the sheriff's department as well as in the station. I said I'd look for a job, maybe apply at B of A in Oxnard. So, the plan was on.

We moved into a two-bedroom apartment on Oxnard Beach. But within nine months, I realized it wasn't going to work. I am confused on what happened to lead up to that decision, but it was mutual. My attentions weren't on him, and his weren't on me. We called it quits once again. It was over. No more. I gave it a go, he gave it a go, and it didn't work out.

Barry and I moved to Mamaw's house, temporarily, in El Rio; Jim moved back to Camarillo. He took the Camaro convertible and the payments. I was fine with that. My uncle Lee sold me a 1950 Oldsmobile, one of those vintage boxy four-door vehicles. Fifty dollars. Ha Ha. Loved it.

Uncle Lee was a mechanic on the outskirts of Oxnard, owned a garage where he worked on trucks and cars, from 18-wheelers on down. And he had a small lot on the property to buy and sell used cars. I loved that boxy Olds, and I paid cash for it. So funny. Doesn't take much to make me happy, I'm tellin' ya. Freedom was most important to me then, and it still is.

Bank of America called me in for an interview and they hired me as a teller at their main branch in Oxnard. My grandmother took care of Barry while I worked. Life felt good in the daytime, my secrets were safe. But at night as I lay in bed, the thoughts of remorse were overwhelming. I wanted to tell Mamaw about Tami but couldn't do it because of daddy. He wouldn't want the family to know.

My uncle Bill and my McMullen cousins were rescuers to me, they didn't know about the baby, of course. My cousins Don and Ken would take me out occasionally, I loved being with them. They made me forget my problems. Soon I began dating again.

CHAPTER 10

Other Lovers

ERROL R.

One day while I was working in B of A in Oxnard, Lo and Behold, Errol from Morro Bay strolled in and came right to my teller line. I saw him grinning at me in the lobby, and I, too, grinned from ear to ear. It was so good to see him.

"Why hello, Errol! And what brings you to Oxnard on this gray foggy day?"

He laughed. "I heard you were working here. I see you are pretty as ever." He handed a check and a deposit slip to me.

"And you are as handsome as ever. You on a construction job down here?"

"Yes, for two weeks. Maybe I can take you to dinner on Friday?"

"Sure. I'd love that. I'll give you a number where I can be reached. I'm staying with my grandmother in El Rio. Call me there."

It was thrilling to see Errol again. I needed the familiar. And I was back to better than my old self, weight and size-wise: 124 lbs. and size 6. We had a few dates, lunches and dinners those two weeks, and caught up on the gossip from Cayucos, where he lived. He also brought me up to date about the bank crew in Morro Bay. The bank manager there had told him where I was, that's how he knew I was in Oxnard. I gave my past employer as a reference. Errol and he were good

179

friends; he did a lot of business with Errol and his dad.

It was good to see him, we had a fun time while he was in Oxnard. Some loving moments, some sex, but nothing serious. When his job was done, he went back up north. I didn't see him again until quite a few years later.

No other lovers to speak of before I met second husband after that. There were dates, always dating, but nothing to mention here.

Chapter 11

Husband Number Two

MITCH M.

Mitch immediately caught my eye before he opened the glass doors coming into Bank of America in Oxnard. I was on the front teller line and in walked this ultra-dapper fellow wearing a cravat, believe it or not, which was not usual Oxnard attire in the '60s. In Hollywood or Santa Barbara, yes. He was very cordial and polite, greeted people he knew, I noticed, and reminded

181

me of Fernando Lamas the film star. I didn't know
what nationality Mitch was but thought he might
be something other than the normal. He was tan,
either from ethnicity or the sun. His eyes and hair
were dark, and he had a European look and flair
about him. The new XKE Jaguar which he parked
near the glass doors of the bank set him apart too.
His clothing and shoes were immaculate and
looked expensive. Those were my first
impressions.

He went to another teller's line, stood there
a few moments, then at one point moved over to
mine as it shortened. It was after five on Friday,
payday for most companies, so we were flooded
with customers wanting to cash or deposit their
checks. I think it was a government payday too.
Perhaps a long weekend.

His charm was addicting and something new
for me. I'd not met such a suave man up to then.
As we chit-chatted, I recorded his deposit. In those

days we took deposits and manually processed by making out cash tickets, hand stamping checks, and placing the transaction in a tray to the side for another person to pick up and take to the hand-operated sorting machine.

Mitch smiled at me when the deposit was completed, said goodbye, then left. But he stopped back at the original teller, Suzanne, to speak to her, then he was gone.

After our shift, I asked Suzanne about him, and she said he was a friend of her boyfriend and had helped her move into an apartment the past weekend. Told me Mitch was single and he worked on a ship called the Range Tracker; they sailed to the South Pacific, Midway, Marshall Islands, and other places to track the Gemini missile shots for NASA.

So, when I met him, his job was tracking Gemini missiles from a ship.

Suzanne said, "He's an engineer, that explains the way he dresses."

"I've seen other engineers and they don't look as well-put-together as Mitch or dress like him at all," I replied.

She laughed, "Well, he's good looking, I'll say that. I see him all the time, so I'll tell him you're interested."

"Oh no! No," I said, panicking. "That will embarrass me!"

But she did anyway, and on his next payday when he came into the bank, he brought his fine-looking self directly to my window. I sent an evil eye glance to Suzanne, she just grinned.

During the processing of that deposit and a cash withdrawal, he asked me to dinner the following Saturday, a week away. Said he knew a place in Santa Barbara with excellent food. We could leave in the afternoon and ride along the coastal highway, enjoy the sights with the top down (had a removable hard top and a cloth convertible top).

The restaurant was in Montecito and had a fabulous chateaubriand for two. I didn't know what the heck that was, didn't ask, would look it up later. I wasn't all that worldly at 24. Sure, I'd been married and had a three-year-old son, but my knowledge of foods, travel, events of the world and its people were limited. I'd been all over New Mexico and California, and that was the extent of my travel experience. Inexpensive American and Mexican food was all I'd had up to that point as an adult, nothing fancy, all easy to spell and pronounce.

But I had French, Italian, Chinese, and Basque food in Kern County as a teenager … thanks to daddy. Most Sundays, we had Sunday Dinner out (lunch after church); I loved our family of five outings on Sunday afternoons. But I usually ate the most ordinary staples on the menus, not the

185

exotic and non-American choices. And with first husband Jim, spaghetti and enchiladas were the extent of our foreign foods, Americanized. So come to think if it, that was a pretty good variety by the mid-sixties.

Mitch was quite a romantic man, and his worldly demeanor and knowledge tugged at my heart strings. I can assure you it was Mitch's charm and debonaire manner that reeled me in. I was also transfixed by his talents – art and Spanish guitar playing.

He handled me like no other could. He loved to explain how things were put together and how they worked. He spent hours doing that. At first, I was very interested in what he had to say, but at one point I was tempted to tell him I wasn't into the technical side of everything on the planet. I didn't need to know. He knew about everything. Mention it, and he would tell when it was discovered, how it was made, and all the uses. He was ready to tell me everything about anything, and he did. So very smart! He would have been a terrific teacher!

I looked up Chateaubriand myself, and learned it originally referred to the preparation of the dish, "a large center cut fillet of tenderloin grilled between two lesser pieces of meat that are discarded after cooking." Wow! That's a waste. However, the specific cut of tenderloin was named Chateaubriand by famed chef and restaurateur Auguste Escoffier. And there were several others who are also given the creator rights. (*A side note: I stayed at Hotel Chateaubriand in Saint Malo, France not so long ago. Mitch would have loved it.*)

We had the most elegant dinner at the French Restaurant he chose in Montecito on our first date. Mitch was classic in his blazer and cravat, Italian shoes, silk shirt and gabardine pants … and of course he was charming. He ordered the wine and the works, Baked Alaska for dessert. Didn't ask me diddly squat. Didn't show me the menu. It was a beautiful candle-lit experience. And he told me about his Greek father and a little bit about his ancestors.

We went dancing after dinner in a chandelier lounge nearby. His gentlemanly old-world composure captivated me. Proper etiquette, all the way.

I don't remember where we stayed in Santa Barbara that night, I am sure it was a four or five star hotel. He certainly swept this girl off her feet. Literally. I was in love! There it is again … in love again. Treat me nicely and I will love you forever! Well … not forever. Ha!

Over the next few months, he taught me how to make love, being the teacher that he was, how to relax and try to enjoy it, mainly. This country bumkin was melting in his arms. But I never reached the uninhibited sexual level that he hoped for; total abandonment of my reserved sexual ways didn't happen yet. I relaxed somewhat, though. But not totally. And I found that drinking Vodka Tonics before the act helped. He was a Scotch drinker.

First, he explained the 'missionary style' position. You know, face to face, man on top. He said it was the proper sex position taught by Christian missionaries in the 1940s. I wondered what people called it before the '40s but didn't ask because I was afraid it would kick off a lengthy dissertation. I knew my grandmothers and mother were not creative in bed, so what did they call their stiff lie-on-your-back-and-think-about-something-else position?

Then he taught positions with me on top. I didn't like that.

A few weeks later came oral sex. I balked at that, couldn't get past what I felt was nasty and pornographic. O good Lord! That totally stressed me out. But he was very patient with me, and steadfast, and I succumbed. Like I say, he was a good teacher of the basics.

But in all the years with all the husbands and other lovers, giving oral sex was not my favorite, but taking was okay … although, unfair to take, if you don't give. I'm surprised I didn't have ulcers over this by the '70s. There was a tremendous amount of gratin' going on in my stomach by then.

So, I was on a learning scale over the next few years with Mitch and after Mitch. I learned all the tricks, watched a few porno films and saw strip shows with husbands and a few lovers, read books about how to please a man sexually … and all the while I was still masturbating in secret, doing what I liked best.

Well, it only took us a few months of sex to get me pregnant. Yep, I did it again! We hadn't used protection and I wasn't on the pill. I don't even know if there was such a thing yet.

190

Regardless, what was wrong with my thinking?
What was wrong with his?

He was out on the ship near Kwajalein
Island when I first suspicioned I was pregnant. But
I ignored it, just like last time.

Let's back up a little …

Mitch had previously married the love of his
life and she had died a few months after their
wedding due to a heart ailment that couldn't
support a pregnancy. She died of complications
one week after an approved clinical abortion.
Consequently, when I told Mitch at our
relationship's six-month mark that I thought I was
pregnant, it devastated him. I understand how he
must have felt at the news, having previously gone
through a killer pregnancy with his bride. And I
can understand that he hadn't healed yet from that
devastation, he had said he would never marry

again. My pregnancy complicated things for both of us.

For me, it was too soon behind the tragedy and birthing that I had the year before. I call it a tragedy for several reasons. I hadn't recovered from the heartbreak of those reasons, yet, and wouldn't for years to come.

One would think that I would have taken precaution since giving away a child had been the most traumatic event of my life up till then. But no! Now I was pregnant again and not married. I was old enough to know better. Can't blame it on my youth. What had I been thinking? The first thoughts were 'how could I put my parents through this again?' How could I put myself through it? What the hell was the matter with me?

Well, it didn't matter at that point, I was pregnant, no two ways about it, and Mitch had already said he never wanted to marry again, and he didn't want children. Now I was paying the price for being so stupid.

Surprisingly enough, despite Mitch losing his wife as a result of an abortion, he arranged for me to get an abortion in Mexico, they weren't legal in the US. We drove the five hours to Tijuana to solve both our dilemmas. Yes, I was scared and emotional, but acquiesced against my nature.

But it was terrifying! I can visualize it as if it happened just yesterday. I've never forgotten a moment of it, can still feel it to my core. A nightmare. We met a cab driver, by prior arrangement, on the streets of Tijuana, who insisted we leave Mitch's Jaguar parked on that street, which he refused to do. We both rode in the XKE, following the cabby into the backstreets of the most run-down part of the border town to an old three-story ramshackle wood-framed house: dusty. dirty looking, no plants, shrubs nor trees, barren, paint peeling. Looked like an abandoned house one would see in a ghost town. We climbed the splintered wooden steps up to a wrap-around porch and entered the doors into a so-called "reception area." It was a dowdy parlor.

Mitch stayed in the parlor. I was ushered to another room that once must have been a kitchen, or maybe still was, it could have been, looked like one. A heavy-looking, long wooden table had been placed in the center of the room. I was shaking by that time. Linoleum was rippled and peeling from the floor; a few cabinet doors were hanging lopsided on rusty hinges, some by only one hinge. Unbelievable, but true, I swear! A corner of the room had a drooping curtain drawn across a rope creating a makeshift dressing space.

I was given a wrinkled exam gown that had probably been worn by everybody that week. By then, I was shaking so violently, my teeth rattled. I could hardly take off my clothing to put on the gown. It was an involuntary shaking; I couldn't control it for the life of me. Then I became weepy. My soul was rejecting the decision to abort.

A "nurse" of sorts led me from the dressing area to the table and asked me to step up using a wooden stool and to lie down on the table. She had on a nurse's uniform, so I assumed she was bona-fide. As if all one needs to do to be a nurse is put on a uniform. I noticed that her dark ruby nail polish was chipped, and the matching lipstick that was drawn above her lips had bled into the deep wrinkles. Her dingy white uniform was a bit tight around the bust and belly and it hiked up in the front. I could see the top of her rolled nylons just below her knees. Her black shoes were scuffed; they reminded me of flamenco dancer shoes.

A "doctor" came in - a short fat man, with long dirty fingernails, I spied those right off. Fingernails I always notice on a person, then the eyes. His eyes wouldn't look at mine. His clothing was wrinkled as if picked off the floor from a corner somewhere where they'd lain wadded up in a pile for quite some time. His hair was thick, black, oily and straggly. He hadn't shaven, had a few days of stubble.

It was all so surreal; it gave me a horrific foreboding feeling. I got dizzy. My whimpering continued as the horrid man examined me, pushing his grimy hand up inside me. It is a wonder he didn't wound me with his fingernails. And then again, maybe he did.

He asked how far along I was as he poked around in my cavity.

"Uh … seven months," I lied weakly, for I knew abortions had to be performed early in a pregnancy. Not that it would matter to these people, but then again it might.

It did. They looked at each other and backed off, whispering in a huddle. He turned and left the room.

The nurse said they couldn't perform the abortion; I was too far along. She helped me up and my shaking and weeping increased from relief. All the feelings I had pushed down into the depths of my being began to erupt like a volcano. I sobbed. Loudly. She had to help me get dressed. I shook like a person in shock, couldn't stop shaking, and couldn't control my sobs. I *was* in shock.

I didn't know how the waiting "daddy" would take what had just transpired, the reversal of the decision, and at that point I didn't care. All I knew was that I could not go through with the abortion and there was not going to be another attempt. Saved by the bell! I was going to have my baby and keep it. I was not going to give this one away; I couldn't survive that again. I'd made my bed and now I was going to get in it and pull the covers over my head. To hell with Mitch!

After I wept the five hours back to Oxnard, Mitch dropped me off at my apartment, said goodbye, and we stopped seeing each other. His not wanting to marry me and his obvious disappointment that I didn't go through with the abortion, broke my heart.

Oh, well, I thought. I was glad I had moved in with Suzanne, was paying half the rent in a nice apartment near the bank, where we worked. I had my $50 car that worked like a charm, thanks to my auto mechanic Uncle. So, I would figure it all out. I didn't need Mitch.

Within ten days of the trip to Mexico, I developed an atrocious infection, burning and inflammation; fluid was literally running, not dripping, from me. I couldn't believe it. Nothing had ever happened to me like that before and I was frightened half out of my wits. I wasn't feeling well either, had a temperature, but I was afraid to go to a doctor. I suppose it was because I didn't want the pregnancy to be confirmed just yet. I was thinking maybe it would just go away if I ignored it. Maybe I really wasn't pregnant. But the infection increased and using tampons and using over-the-counter remedies weren't effective.

The doctor I finally saw told me it was the worst case of Chlamydia that he had ever seen. He questioned me and I told him of the near abortion. He said that if there had been a surgical procedure on that abortion table, I most assuredly may have lost my life, the infection would have gotten into my bloodstream. He said that as a result of just the contact with that man's hands and instruments, I was infected beyond belief. He felt we had caught it in time and that it wouldn't affect the baby. Yes, I was pregnant, it wasn't a tumor or a rumor, it was a real live tiny human being living inside of me and I was five months along.

Doc put me on a fourteen-day antibiotic program and with additional self-injected medications, it finally cleared up. But before it was all over, I had more fever, inflammation, abdominal pains, headaches, bleeding, and nausea. Never had I experienced anything like it before nor have I since. It was as if my body was rebelling. Mitch didn't know any of this.

Weeks went by. Working at the bank, I camouflaged my thickening mid-section as well as I could. My co-workers told me later, they had figured I was just gaining weight; had no clue I was pregnant.

When I was nearly seven months along, Mitch called out of the blue one day (hadn't seen or heard from him since he dropped me off after Mexico). He said he wanted to marry me, said we could get married on a lunch break in a judge's chambers. I must say, although still very hurt, I was grateful. I still hadn't told anyone I was pregnant; I'd been avoiding my family. And his offer did imply something about his feelings of responsibility, if nothing else.

After we married in a noontime ceremony in judge's chambers, Mitch left immediately for a few months on the missile tracking ship. When it was time for Micheal to be born, he was still at sea.

Barry and I were visiting my parents in Morro Bay, that Christmas holiday, when my water broke. So, my angel Micheal was born at Sierra Vista hospital in San Luis Obispo, weighing in at nearly nine pounds. I'd been given a saddle block, and ended up with a spinal anesthesia lumbar puncture headache - the headache that surpasses all headaches, migraines included. You literally wish you would die, and you think you are. You can't bear the pain, can't move, can't sit up, can't tolerate light or the least bit of noise, voices hit you like sledgehammers to the head. I was drugged and lay flat on my back for a week in the hospital. Didn't see Micheal or hold him until transported, still prone, still in pain, to my parents' home. It took nearly ten days for the pain to go away. Then I had to deal with the burning blisters from the Iodine that had been painted on my back for the spinal injection. I am allergic to Iodine, as it turns out.

Mitch arrived at my parents the second week and met his first son, who was the spitting image of him. But sad to say, he shocked me by asking if he indeed was the father. Another stab in my heart. These stabs and jabs were chipping away at my respect for Mitch.

But I will say this much, despite all the pain and all the rest of it, I was thrilled to have my adorable son Micheal. He was a dream child, dark hair and eyes, such a loving baby, and a cuddly butter ball. I was so proud of him. He never cried or fussed. You would think that after all he'd gone through inside of me, and all the outer turmoil he must have felt, he would have been affected by it all. But he wasn't. He slept well, he ate well, and he was the perfect baby. The more I adored Micheal, the more the feelings of guilt overwhelmed me about giving up my daughter two years before (she was born January 1964, he was born December 1965).

She should have been there with us, alongside my two sons Barry and Micheal. I loved my babies.

Mitch and I played at being happy husband and wife during those first two years, and most of the time we were all right, at least I was. Some of the original luster had disappeared for me after all that had been spoken and done. The glitter had dulled. Mitch left ships and took a desk job in Human Resources. We moved to Lompoc, bought a house in Vandenberg Village. But he still traveled most of the time – two or three weeks a month - interviewing and hiring for Federal Electric one of the major aerospace contractors to NASA on Vandenberg AFB. I kept busy with Barry and Micheal, and I was working 40 hours a week as a contracts bookkeeper in a furniture store in Lompoc. We used babysitters and preschool for the boys. I really didn't know how Mitch felt about it all, he was away mostly, and besides, he wasn't one to discuss his feelings. But he adored Micheal. He couldn't deny him.

We would have outings and picnics and Sunday drives when Mitch was not traveling. So, it was good for the boys and me too. And Mitch and I would go out to dinner in Vandenberg village where we lived, and with friends to several steak houses in Santa Maria, Casmalia, and Lompoc. Solvang was a few miles down the road too. And I would take the boys and go visit my parents and sisters for weekends on occasion. Sometimes

Mitch would take us, if he was home. Easters, Fourth of Julys, Thanksgivings, Christmases we celebrated as a family. He really was trying to be a family man. He truly was. But it was awkward for him. He was different.

He knew I was afraid of creepy crawlers and the dark. It was funny to him when he would catch a grasshopper and tie a string around it and hop it after me through the house. The boys would get it kick out of it too. Harmless, yes. But when he deliberately tried to scare me in the dark, that was another story.

One time when he returned from a trip, unexpectedly after midnight, I was sound asleep. He crept in quietly. I felt a presence and woke up to Mitch's face a couple inches above mine, lit up with a flashlight under his chin, with his bugged eyes and teeth showing. Scared me so much, my body raised up in bed, he said. And I fainted.

205

Terrifying. After that I left the lights on all night when he was away.

Mitch's job as a recruiter, took him out of town at least two weeks a month, sometimes three weeks. So, I worked forty hours a week at the furniture store and kept the home fires burning those first two years in Lompoc.

One day I found a little pocket notebook in his dresser drawer while cleaning and organizing. The notebook was an account Mitch had been logging my supposed activities when he was out of town before Micheal was born. He had drawn charts of the months marking my period dates. There were questions such as: curly hairs not hers in bathtub? Unanswered phone calls? Lunch dates? Time took after work to get home? And he had listed his suspicions under the questions. There were others too, but I remember these especially. That explains his asking whether Micheal was his when he returned after Micheal was born. I couldn't believe he had been doing that. Poor soul!

I threw the notebook at him when he came through the door, and said, "Ridiculous!" No more said about it.

I became pregnant again. There were only three short years between our second son Mark's birth and death. He died a month after his third birthday. I feel a knot in my stomach that is rising to my throat as I write this. I try to blink away the blurriness in my eyes to hold back the deluge I know is coming, always, when I think of Mark's death. Fifty years have passed, and it still hurts.

Mark would have been fifty-four years old three days before this upcoming Christmas. Would his blond hair still be blond? His blue eyes, still blue? Just the opposite of his brother Micheal, same as his half-brother Barry. Would Mark still have the classic Greek cleft in his chin same as his father? Yes, Mark was a blond, blue-eyed little

Greek-Scottish boy who loved to sing and giggle, and everybody adored him.

Every year on his December birthday, I try to visualize him a year older. But when I look at his tiny red-trimmed, blue quilted jacket that is hanging by its hood on my library door, for the life of me I can't imagine him any bigger than that little jacket. I don't see him as a fifty-four-year-old man. He's only three. Micheal wore that little jacket, too. First it belonged to Micheal then to Mark.

I remember the chaos and bitterness in my marriage while I was pregnant with Mark. None of it was because of him or his older brothers. My unhappiness was never because of my children who were always my joy and delight. (Even though I feel I neglected them in their teens, due to my focus on work and new husbands.) My unhappiness was with the men in my life over the years, has always been about the men. It is the choices I make for me; you see. I take all the blame.

When I became pregnant with Mark, it was a crazy time during that pregnancy, too. Our marriage took a turn for the worse. Mitch still worked for the government contractor in the aerospace industry and his days and nights away had increased even more. It was as if my being pregnant pushed him away.

I've always attributed the fact that we lasted nearly ten years to his travel, and of course, to the death of Mark. If Mark hadn't died, I feel I'd have eventually taken my babies and left sooner than I did. In fact, I'd retained a divorce attorney and had planned to do just that, the week before the death of little Mark.

But first, I want to back up here …

I remember two instances when I was eight months pregnant with Mark that should have been enough for me to pack up and leave before he was born.

Now, I know I can be a stinker too, yes, I know that. And I feel I do bring most of my head and heartache onto myself. If I'd stayed home like a nice little pregnant wife this one night, then what followed never would have happened. But I was lonely. I was bored. I felt neglected. I was eight months pregnant.

It felt as if my husband didn't care a nickel about me or even like me (caused, no doubt, by a pregnant woman's hormone imbalance, and the unresolved feelings of before). This night Mitch went bowling, he substituted on a team. Also at the bowling alley was the most popular bar and live music lounge in town, with dancing. So, I wanted to go with him to listen to the music if nothing else, but he insisted I stay home. So, I did. For a while, that is, being the independent cuss that I am.

I got a babysitter and called a cab an hour after he left. I figured I'd ride home with him.

Into the bowling alley I went to surprise Mitch and was feeling happy and excited about it. But to my own surprise, he was cozying up to another female. Later, he said she was doing the cozying, he wasn't doing anything. I just stood there and watched for a few minutes, and then I let my presence be known. I suppose I was a bit over-reactive, and we'll just leave it at that. Beware of the wrath of a pregnant woman scorned. Lordy.

After a few words, I turned and went out of the door into the night and began walking home because I didn't have money for another cab, and I wasn't going to ask him for one red cent. Again, my choice, my bad judgment. It was six miles to our house in Vandenberg Village from the Lompoc bowling alley. I walked the first three miles and was beginning to feel as if I couldn't walk any further when a car pulled to the side of the road

211

ahead of me, and a stranger asked if I needed a ride. He said he'd seen me when he came into town and now that he was going back home to Vandenberg AFB, he was startled that I was still walking in my condition. This was nearly 11:00 p.m. He recognized my hesitancy and convinced me that I shouldn't fear him. I took a chance; at that point I didn't really care. I just couldn't walk another step and I was cold. He took me home, I was safe.

So, you see if I hadn't gone to the bowling alley, that wouldn't have happened. But it was the foreshadowing of things to come. I truly believe you put yourself in line for what happens to you. If you suspect the worst, the worst will happen. What you put out into the universe will come back at you in spades.

Another night before I gave birth to Mark, I returned from spending a week with my sister in

Shafter, near Bakersfield. The exact day of my return had been undecided and when I got home, I tried to reach Mitch by phone, but he was nowhere to be found. No cell phones then. Finally, one of our young widow gal pals told me he was at a party and that he'd invited her to go. She wanted to know if I wanted to ride with her. So, I hired a babysitter, and I went with her to the house party.

When we arrived, the lights were out, but there were lots of cars parked up and down the street. The front door was ajar, so in we went without ringing the doorbell. The house was packed with couples kissing, talking, drinking, cuddling, etc. Off in one room they were watching porno flicks, music and dancing in another. It was dark, but one could make out the faces and forms. I didn't see Mitch.

We walked into the kitchen and there he was, in an embrace with his secretary, or what appeared to be an embrace. He had her backed up against the kitchen sink, with both arms around her. And I recognized his inebriated sway. They were both swaying with their bodies pressed together. I was shaken. The adrenaline rushed to my head, and I stepped forward and tapped him on the shoulder.

He told me to go home. I left.

My gal pal and I drove around as I fumed and fussed. Finally, I said I wanted to go back. She advised against it, but I insisted. So here we go, again, I could have avoided what happened next. You get what you ask for, remember. There was no reason for me to go back. I saw all I needed to see. I was about to have my fourth baby; I needed to go home and make plans to divorce Mitch.

When we walked through the front door this time, Mitch was lying on the living room floor in front of the fireplace, on top of his secretary. They were kissing.

I kicked his foot and told him I was going to go home and throw his clothing out of the house, and he could pick it all up from the front lawn and go stay at so-and-so's house and she could do his laundry and cooking forever!

He slowly got up and came towards me, eyes half closed with drunkenness, and pushed me out of the house.

"You son of a bitch!" I screamed.

He drew back and cold-cocked me. Decked me. K.O.'d me.

How was I to know how personal he would take what I said? I am kidding, I did know. He'd told me about a woman he walloped when she called him an SOB years before, when he was in the Air Force in Korea. But then … a man should not strike a woman, unless his life is in danger at the hand of that woman. I was not a physical threat to him. I may have wished him dead, but that doesn't make it so.

As I came to, I heard voices saying, "help her, help her." I felt a mist on my face, it had been a foggy day and there were forecasts of a December rainstorm coming through. Then I felt actual raindrops. I was still lying on my back on the sidewalk. I can imagine how I looked … an eight-month pregnant woman, a big blob of a woman, being doused by the rain, face beginning to swell. Then one of the other women and my dear friend tried to help me up.

I was still dazed when I said 'Besse, please take me home."

Mitch intervened, "She'll ride with me." He pushed them aside and took me to his car.

We went home. No words were exchanged. I went right to bed. He took care of the babysitter.

Because of the facial injury, swelling and discoloration, I missed a week of work. My employer and his assistant manager, bless them, came to the house and wanted me to press charges. I said no.

Now, I am not excusing the behavior of Mitch, that's something he had to pay for in the long run, and probably did, but I am aware of how I could have handled the situation to avoid confrontation. Again, you go looking for trouble, you'll find it. I hadn't learned that, yet. My advice to others, extract yourself immediately. That was the one and only time he hit me. But it did its damage to our relationship. It was the beginning of the end.

We were in a marriage that had started out all wrong, that wasn't destined to be, and there was no getting around it. Unfortunately, I remained in it as long as I did. But then again, it brought me two beautiful babies and of that I was grateful. They were the blessings of that marriage. My time with those children was well worth it.

The next three years, Barry, Micheal and Mark were loving brothers. Barry had neighbor friends his age, Micheal and Mark played together all the time, being only two years apart, and both were "good" boys. They hardly did anything they weren't supposed to, were well-behaved in public and I just couldn't hold them and love on them enough, it seemed. I missed them all when I was working, although most of the time Mitch and I were out and about at least three nights a week, socializing when he was home. But I still managed to spend quality time with my sons, all three of them, and we had some precious times together at home and on holiday outings.

Mitch and I weren't getting along at all, and our pretense marriage was almost over.

Then, the time with Mark was tragically cut short one month after his third birthday. He ate a container of my pills.

There was no anecdote to the anti-depressant Norpramin, overdosage caused death.

I'd taken one pill of the prescribed medication —Norpramin —and was wide-awake for 48 hours. So, I didn't take any more of it, set it on the top shelf of the medicine cabinet. I wasn't depressed anyway. I was unhappy. I knew that. And I knew why I was unhappy. I wanted out of the marriage. So, I decided not to take the pills, I don't do well with prescribed meds. What I should have done was flush them down the toilet, but I didn't. Shoulda coulda woulda.

I do want to interject here, however, that not only did Mitch have extramarital dalliances; I had one a few months earlier, before tragedy struck. Bert (yes, dear, dear Bert) had telephoned me to wish me happy birthday in September, we both had September birthdays, and I'd begun writing him letters about how I felt about my marriage to

Mitch, how I wanted to divorce him. Bert asked if I'd be able to join him at the design expo coming up in L. A. So, I reconnected with my high school love, once again. We spent two nights together in Los Angeles, while Mitch was on a recruiting trip. I fell in love all over again with Bert and I decided to leave Mitch as soon as I could. In fact, that was what prompted my filing for divorce while Mitch was away that December.

On the fatal evening in January, Mark had discovered my prescription of pills on the top shelf of the medicine cabinet as he curiously nosed around on one of his trips to the master bathroom. He found and had eaten the remaining candy-coated pills.

Afterwards, he came into the bedroom, next to the bathroom, and jumped up on the bed with me. I was watching TV, Mitch was in San

Francisco, recruiting and processing new hires to man a project in Thailand.

"Mommy, I ate all your candy pills," Mark said in a sing-song voice as he grinned widely, as if it was the best thing in the world he could do.

"You did what?"

"I ate your candy pills." He was giggly and excited.

"Show me!" I got up and led him into the bathroom.

He climbed up on the counter, stood up and opened the medicine cabinet above the sink, and took the container from the top shelf and handed it to me, still grinning. He had emptied it and replaced the lid and put it back on the top shelf. The prescription was for 24 pills, I'd taken only one.

"I dropped one," he said as he pointed to the deep shag rug that was on the bathroom floor.

I dropped to my knees and ran my hands furiously through the rug, hoping to find more than one surviving pill, deducing how many he'd taken. I panicked. Didn't find any. I telephoned the pediatrician. He wasn't familiar with the drug, but suggested I get Mark to vomit by having him drink lots of water, and then holding a table knife on his tongue to gag him. I was to call him back, if anything developed.

We vomited several times, Mark did, and I felt like I did too, right along with him.

Mitch had been in San Francisco for a month. So, I told Mark he could sleep with me while he was gone. Micheal was five years old and sleeping in their room. Barry was nine years old and in his own bedroom.

About an hour after Mark fell asleep, he awoke abruptly and wildly jumped up and down on the bed a couple of times, and then started to run through the house, screaming. I ran after him, caught him and brought him back to bed, him fighting me the whole time. I couldn't understand what was happening. I yelled out to Barry for help. Suddenly Mark bent backwards in my arms, in an incredible, odd arch and stiffened. It was a seizure. I couldn't get a response from him. I ran carrying him to the nurse that lived next door. Couldn't remember her phone number to call her. It was after midnight.

But it was too late. Mark was dead. He was gone. My bright-eyed, fun-loving baby, who laughed and sang and talked up a blue streak, was dead in my arms.

I felt my entire world go black. I couldn't see anything around me or in the past or future, all I could see in my mind's eye was Mark and those final moments when he had the seizure and died. I relived it over and over for months. Today I still see and feel it. I cried till there were no more tears, and then I cried without the tears. I didn't think I'd ever survive his death. I didn't want to. And the guilt piled on me again: my dalliance with Bert, not disposing of the prescription when I quit taking the pills, not calling my doctor instead of the pediatrician. But my doctor called me a couple days later to assure me that nothing could have been done. No anecdote.

The year that followed just happened. For months I was a zombie. I drifted through it and felt nothing, said nothing, no opinions, no feelings. People had stopped mentioning Mark to me for fear of making me weep, which it would. It took many more years for me to be able to talk about Mark without crying, although the tears still come even now.

When a mother loses a child, it is devastating. Whether that loss is through a long illness, sudden or accidental death, adoption, through divorce, wars, what have you, there isn't anything, and I will repeat, *nothing* compares to a mother's love for her children … and a child's love for a mother … or a brother's love for a brother. And I lost two, Tami and Mark, by the time I was 34.

It goes without saying that Barry, Mitch and Micheal were also deeply affected by the loss and mourned in their own ways; however, I am writing this from my perspective.

It wasn't long after that, we made a life change. By the way I didn't go through with the divorce.

First Mitch's immediate boss quit the aerospace company and moved to Houston, Texas and went to work for the Bonanza steakhouse chain. He talked Mitch into doing the same. So, we sold the house and moved to Texas a year after Mark died. We lived in Houston a year, and then Mitch was promoted to Dallas headquarters to run the training program for new managers. We were in Dallas a year when Mitch decided he wanted to open his own restaurant in Morro Bay.

In Houston I was hired by the Miss Charm national beauty pageant as general manager, and in Dallas I bought a four-string guitar and taught myself how to play and I wrote some songs. Was good for me, I kept busy.

We moved back to California, after two years in Texas, to Morro Bay where Mitch decided to build a motel, shops and a restaurant on the waterfront. An ambitious undertaking.

We rented a little house, and I went into business with my sister. She and I opened a shop downtown Morro Bay, called Marbeck's – a combination of our first names (Mary + Becky).

Property on the waterfront, Mitch optioned for his complex. He paid an architect to draw up elevation plans to be approved, and then it all fell through when the Coastal Commission didn't approve before year's end and our financial backers withdrew. They needed to dump their money before the end of the year for tax purposes.

So, Mitch went back to work for the aerospace company at Vandenberg, and they sent him right away to Point Barrow, Alaska, to man a project.

After he was in Alaska for six months, Mitch wanted me and the boys to move there. He had been offered the project manager position at Point Barrow. I said no that I was in business in Morro Bay, and I liked it there. And we ended up getting a divorce and sold two undeveloped lots that we still had in Lompoc, split the proceeds.

We went our merry ways. I stayed in Morro Bay in the shop partnership with my sister Mary and was happy to be living near family once again. Barry, Micheal, and me.

There were many more hurdles ahead after divorce. I was 35 years old.

EPILOGUE

What's Next?

Two down, first two husbands I married and divorced - Jim and Mitch, six to go.

Those two were like night and day, so different from each other - looks, manner, socially, intellectually, conversation, sexually, in all ways they were total opposites. If I were to search for a common thread, a similarity between them, I'd say none exist, other than they were male.

But going forward, I was so happy to be free from marriage once again. I had no ill feelings, despair or regret for divorcing either of them. I didn't mope or complain to others. Never badmouthed them to our sons.

Sure, there were good times we shared together AND some not so good. But I will always remember them as the men I once loved, my first two husbands, the fathers of my sons (including 'other lover' Ron P., the father of my daughter). I am grateful for the joyous memories, but sad, very sad for the bad.

During the time period 1955 to 1975, in this book, I made some regretful decisions that chipped away pieces of my heart, as well as the hearts of others. I am very, very sorry for that. Specifically, the loss of two babies that took big chunks of my heart with them, leaving holes that will never heal completely. I've never totally recovered from the trauma of either, although a partial healing came years later with one.

I truly feel those losses caused it to be even more difficult to give myself wholeheartedly, to totally commit to anyone in the future. Nothing seemed important and lasting after that. And I'd venture to say I just couldn't comprehend the definition of soulmate love and the total commitment required for a marital relationship to last. I had brain block. Maybe heart block. I don't believe I ever tore down those block walls. But I certainly tried relationships, over and over. I came close a few times, but no cigar … as the saying goes.

The consolation besides my children? I did have some new unforgettable happy experiences in those twenty years and learned that adulthood was much more complicated than teen-hood. Also learned that life was not a fairytale happily-ever-after. I was now an adult in the real world at 35 years of age. Ready to tackle come what may, though not truly ready.

So, join me in the next 'seasons and episodes' of my story, it isn't over yet. It goes on through even more complex times with six more husbands and a bunch of other lovers. Mustn't forget those other lovers, for they were instrumental to my evolvement and decision making too, as you'll see. Confusion galore! Ha!

You may be wondering which one of my husbands was my favorite, or the love of my life. Or was it one of the lovers who I didn't marry? By the end of this tale in Book Four, I think you will guess who they were. Regardless, I will tell you … 1) who was my favorite, and 2) who was my soulmate. I haven't expressed either before. Not even to them, sad to say it is too late now. How about a do over? Sure, Rebecca.

But life goes on, of course, to what we call new beginnings, and of course new people to meet, new places to see … more books to write!

Book Two is scheduled to be published at the end of Summer 2022.

RJ Buckley

Mama & Papa Dearmore   Mamaw & Dad McMullen

Daddy and Mother & Sister Mary

High School Years - 1955 to 1958

TEEN LOVES:

Paul Bergen

Bert Brooks

RJ Buckley

First Marriage – Jim Isom & Son Barry

1958 to 1962

Jim's Parents and Sister

Sister Mary's Wedding During This Time

Second Marriage – Mitch Manos – 1965 to 1975

Sons Mike & Mark

Sister Martha's Wedding During This Time

Mark Ray Manos (b.1967 d.1971)

RJ Buckley

COMING NEXT!

BOOK TWO: 1975 – 1985

Two More of the Eight Husbands

** GARY and JERRY **

& Other Lovers

www.rebeccabuckley.com

rebeccajbuckley@aol.com

RJ Buckley

OTHER BOOKS BY REBECCA BUCKLEY

Midnight Novels (series)

Midnight at Trafalgar

Midnight at the Eiffel

Midnight in Brussels

Midnight in Moscow

Midnight in Malibu

Midnight in Vegas

Novellas

The Christmas Diary

Short Story Collections

Love Has a Price Tag

Bits & Pieces of Me

Shoe's on the Other Foot - eBook only

Stage & Screenplays Collection

My Dramedy

RJ Buckley